Charlie Brown
and
Charlie Schulz

Sparky's first published drawing—when he was 15 years old.

Charlie Brown & Charlie Schulz

By Lee Mendelson
in association with
Charles M. Schulz

In celebration of
the 20th anniversary
of Peanuts

THE WORLD PUBLISHING COMPANY
New York and Cleveland

Published by The World Publishing Company
Published simultaneously in Canada by
Nelson, Foster & Scott Ltd.

SECOND PRINTING— 1970

Copyright © 1970 by United Feature Syndicate, Inc.

All rights reserved

Library of Congress catalog card number: 75–107642

Printed in the United States of America

WORLD PUBLISHING
TIMES MIRROR

For Barbara, Glenn, and Linda

Contents

Prologue

THE phone next to our bed rang loudly.

As I groped for the receiver in the darkness, I noted with horror that the illuminated alarm clock announced that it was ten minutes to six in the morning . . . on Sunday!

I picked up the receiver, said a very weak "Hello," and heard the phone click abruptly on the other end.

I fell back into bed and was asleep within ten seconds.

Again!—a piercing ring from the phone. I noted, as I grabbed for the receiver, that the clock now read just five minutes to six. Angrily I said, *"Yes? Who is this?"* And again, a fast click as the caller hung up immediately.

Then, at intervals of no more than thirty seconds, this same scene was repeated over and over again—each time the caller would hang up as soon as I answered.

My wife Barbara answered a few of the calls, to see if there would be a different response, but she heard the same clicks.

By six-fifteen, after about twenty calls, we started to get a little upset. We'd had quite a bit of publicity lately, especially in connection with the Charlie Brown television specials which we had recently produced with Bill Melendez.

And we were afraid that some cranks—or worse—were trying to scare us.

I decided to take the phone off the hook and to think what we might do next. While thinking that perhaps we should call the police, I put on my robe and went outside to get the Sunday paper, a weekend habit that not even the disturbing phone calls could break.

The Sunday *San Francisco Chronicle* was covered, as usual, by the comic strip section, with *Peanuts* on the front.

As I slowly walked back to the house, I read *Peanuts*, a ritual that I

had practiced years before I had known or worked with Charles Schulz.

The strip that particular day was the one on the preceding page.

As usual, I laughed out loud—but then I stopped short! That telephone number was very familiar. *Very* familiar. In fact, *it was our telephone number!*

What followed—for the next two days and nights—was, for us, remarkable. The phone rarely stopped ringing. We heard from children and adults—from age four to over eighty—from all over northern California.

As we started to answer the phone more cheerfully, the callers stopped hanging up, and they started to talk and to ask questions:

"Is Charlie Brown *really* there?"

"Who lives here, please?"

"Can I please speak to Snoopy?"

"Is this really Charlie Brown?"

I guess some of the children really hoped to hear Charlie Brown, and even some of the adults enjoyed the fantasy of the call. But most of them apparently just wanted to get "involved," just wanted to see who might answer, just wanted to find out what would happen if they dared to ring that phone number.

We heard from all types of people—a policeman in Sausalito, a soldier just returned from Vietnam, a little boy who said his name was really Charles Brown, an infielder (he said) from the San Francisco Giants, a lady celebrating her eighty-second birthday in Oakland, a small girl from a hospital bed in San Mateo—a seemingly endless list of people from all walks of life.

All of the conversations were most pleasant, and our family finally had to work in "shifts" during meals.

Once my daughter Linda, who was then five, answered one of the calls. When the little boy at the other end said, "Is Charlie Brown there?," Linda answered, "No, but this is Lucy . . . can I help you?" and the phone slammed down immediately at the other end.

Before these calls, I naturally had been aware of the tremendous impact of *Peanuts* in everything from the comic strip itself to international success in books to network television. But I was frankly surprised by the general outpouring of good feelings and of good humor by these dozens of people, who, in a sense, believed in the reality of poor old Charlie Brown. It was at this point that I decided to explore the phenomenal world of Charlie Brown and Charlie Schulz and to collect the items describing the worldwide impact of *Peanuts.*

And it now seems fitting—in this the twentieth anniversary year of Charlie Brown—to present a "scrapbook" of my three-year exploration.

Lee Mendelson
Burlingame, California
June 1970

1

Charlie Brown
B̶i̶
alias
Charles
Schulz

ONCE upon a time—about forty-eight years ago—a baby remarkably resembling Charlie Brown is born in St. Paul, Minnesota.

The baby's father—a St. Paul barber—names him Charles Monroe Schulz. But an uncle nicknames him "Sparky" —after "Sparkplug" in the comic strip *Barney Google*—and the name sticks.

In kindergarten and in first grade, Sparky shows an amazing aptitude for drawing. And in other subjects as well, he far exceeds his fellow classmates.

As a result, he is promoted—jumped ahead—two elementary grades. On that occasion, Charlie Brown is "born."

Because of his rapid promotion, Sparky is suddenly the youngest and smallest in his class. He is either ignored or rebuffed by the older, bigger children.

When his classmates pick sides for sporting events, Sparky—because he is so small—is always picked last—or not at all. When the children hold birthday parties, Sparky is usually not invited.

Consequently, he becomes a "loner" —working alone, playing alone, and even eating lunch alone in the school yard . . .

Also, because of the rapid jump ahead, Sparky's grades start to suffer, and his scholastic struggle is to plague him throughout high school. Still the smallest, youngest, and shyest in his class, Sparky manages to flunk at least one subject each year.

Only his great desire for Art—for drawing—seems to sustain him. In his senior year, he submits some sketches for the high school yearbook. The editors say that they will use the sketches. On the last day of school, Sparky excitedly thumbs through the yearbook . . .

. . . but as a symbolic climax to twelve long years of frustration, he discovers that—at the last minute—the sketches have not been used . . .

Too discouraged to continue a formal education after high school, Charles Schulz answers a newspaper advertisement—and enrolls in a correspondence course with Art Instruction Schools of nearby Minneapolis. Of course it was by mail.

But after twenty years of being ignored by practically everybody, suddenly Charles Schulz is in great demand . . .

Nothing less than World War II could have brought this about. Nevertheless, Sparky is drafted into the Army . . .

I WANT YOU

Returning to St. Paul after the war, Sparky is now ready to conquer the cartooning world. Only the world is not ready to cooperate. For over a year, Sparky tries to find art work in the Minneapolis-St. Paul area, but he is turned down . . . time and time again . . . by newspapers and magazines.

Then he gets his first break . . . a small job lettering the balloons of other comic pages. And then another break—Art Instruction Schools hires Sparky as a part-time instructor. And, finally, a St. Paul newspaper starts to run his comic panel—*Li'l Folks*—as a once-a-week feature . . .

Li'l Folks
BY SPARKY

"HI!"

"'RAIN, RAIN, GO AWAY... COME AGAIN SOME OTHER DAY!'"

"IT GOES WITHOUT SAYING THAT MY MERE PRESENCE HERE INDICATES I MUST BE OUT OF MY MIND!"

"I'VE ALWAYS ADMIRED HIM... HE'S SO CAREFREE.."

And to his astonishment, the *Saturday Evening Post* buys one of his cartoons—a simple drawing of a little boy using a footstool that he obviously doesn't need.

As the *Post* runs a few more Schulz cartoons, and as his confidence rises, Sparky marches into the St. Paul newspaper and demands that his weekly feature be increased to a daily feature.

And . . . in the true tradition of Charlie Brown . . . he is FIRED! ! !

Sparky decides to take a "thousand-to-one" shot, and he bundles up his best work and submits it to United Feature Syndicate in New York City. One of the leading syndicates in the world, United receives hundreds of "would-be" comic strips each year, but only one strip in a thousand ever makes a newspaper comic page.

However, United likes what it sees from Charles Monroe Schulz of St. Paul, Minnesota, and the syndicate decides to gamble with poor old Charlie Brown. Thus in 1950, United Feature names the comic strip *Peanuts* and it's introduced in eight newspapers across the United States.

And the success of *Peanuts* is to be the most phenomenal story in comic strip history! ! !

1100-1107

UNITED
FEATURE
SYNDICATE, Inc.

•

METROPOLITAN
NEWSPAPER FEATURE
SERVICE, Inc.

•

WORLD FEATURE SERVICE

2

The Fabulous Funnies

WHAT is this world of comic strips into which Charlie Brown gingerly stepped in 1950?

And what is so special about Charlie Brown that destined him to become the most famous comic strip character of all time?

We found some of the answers to these questions when we produced an hour television special, *The Fabulous Funnies*, featuring most of the top cartoonists of the past half century.

The facts we discovered while writing that show—plus subsequent research—reveal a fascinating record for these fabulous funnies.

The comics are as uniquely American as jazz and Thanksgiving. Having started with *The Yellow Kid* in 1895, the funnies are celebrating their seventy-fifth anniversary this year as America's longest-running "pop culture."

The comics are now read every day by an estimated audience of 100 million Americans, and they are enjoyed by countless millions around the world.

When newspapers conduct polls of their readers, it is rare that the comic strips do not lead the poll as the "most-read" section of the paper.

The funnies have contributed dozens of words and phrases to the English language, such as "Egad" (Major Hoople) ; "Oh-mi-gosh" (Andy Gump) ; "Well blow me down" (Popeye) ; "Balls-a-fire" (Snuffy Smith) ; "Hot Stuff" (Yellow Kid) ; "Good grief" (Charlie Brown) ; one cartoonist alone —T.A.D.—contributed "Twenty-three skidoo," "Apple Sauce," "Ball and Chain," "Cat's Pajamas," and, perhaps the most famous of all, "Hot Dog."

And look what Popeye did for spinach, Wimpy for hamburgers, Dagwood for the sandwich, and Jiggs for corned beef and cabbage!

And, too, the comics have been translated successfully into every form of show business, from the days of vaudeville, when cartoonists like Harry Hershfield did chalk talks on the two-a-day circuit . . . through the Golden Age of Radio, where such programs as "Blondie" and "Little Orphan Annie" were always among the top-rated shows . . . to legitimate stage hits such as *Li'l Abner* and *You're a Good Man, Charlie Brown* . . . through many popular songs, such as "Barney Google with His Goo Goo Googly Eyes" and "Jubilation T. Cornpone" . . . to television (*Dennis the Menace* and *Charlie Brown*).

Somehow, the public so identifies with these fictional characters that their translation to "live" or "animated" form is completely acceptable. In fact, much of America has frequently been caught up in the "reality" of the comic strips: with the birth of Baby Dumpling to Blondie and Dagwood, with the marriage of B. O. Plenty and Gravel Gertie, with the "invasion" of the Shmoos, with the marriage of Li'l Abner and Daisy Mae. Tens of thousands of letters and gifts poured into the studios of cartoonists for these and dozens of other comic strip "happenings" over the past three quarters of a century.

Why have the comics been so popular for so long for so many people?

First, I believe, the funnies have endured because, for the most part, they are pure entertainment. Whether involved with comedy, mystery, adventure, or fantasy, the comics are always entertainment—they rarely take themselves too seriously.

Next, the funnies, as Charles Schulz has frequently stated, are a "sidewalk medium" . . . they appeal to the common man, the so-called man-in-the-street. And they do this basically by using simple drawings and simple language, with plots that are easy to follow. In the frantic pace of the increasingly complex twentieth century, somehow the comics have never lost their "cool," have never lost their leisurely pace.

But perhaps the key to the success of the most famous comic strips is that they have often reflected simply and directly the changing American scene . . . they have often been a mirror of ourselves:

As tens of thousands of immigrants poured into the United States in the 1890's and early 1900's, they inspired the first comic strip character— *The Yellow Kid*—with his nightshirt messages and his language "of the streets" . . .

... followed by the German dialect of the *Katzenjammer Kids* ...

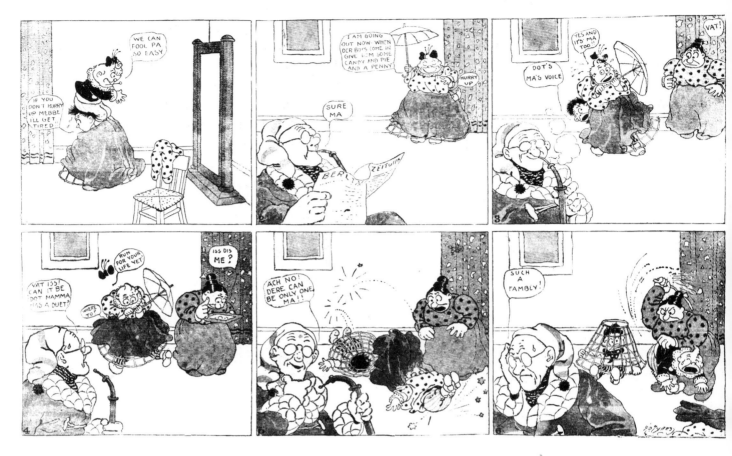

In the following decade, as many of the immigrants suddenly became prosperous, *Bringing Up Father* symbolized the new rich ... and their social-climbing wives.

In 1912, as women fought for their voting rights and for their independence, such strips as *Polly and Her Pals* reflected the emancipation of the American woman . . .

During World War I, as Americans became involved with the rest of the world for the first time and started to become more involved with themselves as well, the first so-called "intellectual" strip, with social comment, caught the nation's fancy . . . the world-famous *Krazy Kat* . . .

After the war, the newfangled motorcars inspired one of the most beloved comic strips of all time—*Gasoline Alley*—starring the Wallet Family . . .

During these same Roaring Twenties, comic strips such as *Moon Mullins* portrayed the pursuit of wealth, of fame, and of glory.

The great sports heroes of the twenties and thirties inspired Ham Fisher to create *Joe Palooka*, the all-American hero, and the gangland wars and corruption of the thirties inspired cartoonist Chester Gould to create—in 1931—the world-famous *Dick Tracy* . . .

And during the Great Depression, as Americans sought escape from the miseries of daily life, they quickly embraced such action strips as *Terry and the Pirates*, the very prophetic *Buck Rogers*, *Tarzan*, and *Prince Valiant* . . .

And in the forties, World War II could create everything from a *Steve Canyon* to a *Beetle Bailey* . . .

. . . to the political satire of *Li'l Abner* and *Pogo* . . .

So what did Charlie Brown and Charles Schulz bring to the comic strips in 1950 that was so different?

How did Charlie Brown reflect the changing American scene of the 1950's and 1960's?

Initially, Sparky employed many of the fundamentals we have just described of comic strips as a whole: simple language, simple drawings, a repertory group of characters, with a basic goal of "entertainment." In addition, however, there were some unique aspects to the strip: a dog with shockingly introspective thoughts; communication between children, sometimes at the children's level and sometimes at what had previously been considered an adult level. Here was a cartoonist at work who was a "bell-ringer," somebody who was reminding us of things in our own childhood that most of us had long forgotten, somebody who was pointing out to us some of the pangs and frustrations of adulthood as well. But was all this a reflection of a changing America? Let me quote a few passages from *Love and Will*, a fascinating book by the brilliant psychiatrist-author, Rollo May:

. . . thus at the annual convention of the American Psychopathological Association in 1949 on the theme "Anxiety," the concept of normal anxiety was still denied by most of the psychiatrists and psychologists who attended.

But in the 1950's a radical change became evident; everyone was talking about anxiety and there were conferences on the problem on every hand. The concept of normal anxiety gradually became accepted in psychiatric literature. Everybody, normal as well as neurotic, seemed to be aware that he was living in the *age of anxiety.*

And who became *Mr. Anxious* of the 1950's and 1960's?

And as Dr. May also states:

. . . our next issue is identity. This was first a concern of therapists in the late 1940's and early 1950's. But in the later 50's and 60's it was on every sophisticated person's lips . . .

And in the late sixties *identity* became important to the man-in-the-street—in the struggles between blacks and whites, parents and children, teachers and students, husbands and wives, flower children and the Establishment.

And who was our greatest seeker of identity in the 1950's and 1960's???

In short, Charlie Brown has become *the* symbol of mid-century America not only because of his great humor but also because Charlie Brown is— as were his most famous comic strip predecessors—a basic reflection of his time. People everywhere have a new awareness of feelings, a need to communicate, and a need to struggle against what often appear to be insurmountable problems. And in the face of these essentially subjective experiences, we struggle with "anxiety," "identity," and "self." Who leads us in this fight? We believe it is poor old Charlie Brown.

And now on the twentieth anniversary of *Peanuts*, we can look back, with Charles Schulz, on Charlie Brown's two decades of struggle, and see how they came to represent so many of the feelings of so many people.

Says Schulz: "I was a real comic strip

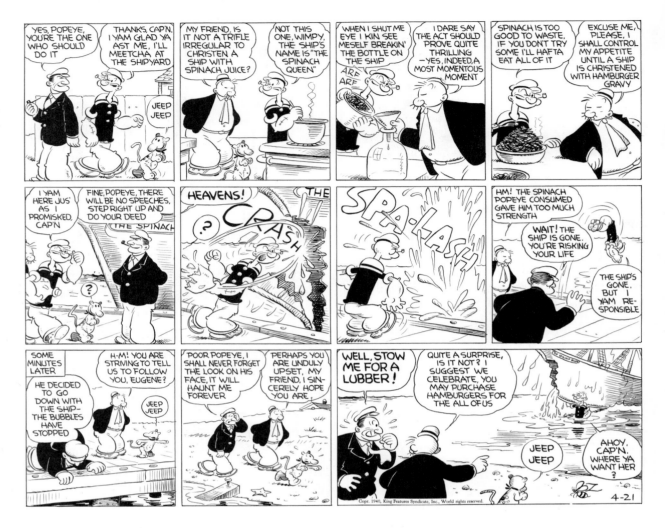

fanatic as I was growing up. In St. Paul, we subscribed to both local newspapers. We always made sure that we went to the drugstore on Saturday night to buy the Minneapolis Sunday papers so that we would be able to read every comic published in the area. At that time, I was a great fan of Buck Rogers, Popeye, and Skippy. I remember always trying to walk by the windows of the St. Paul *Pioneer Press* (when I had a delivery job after high school) so I could watch the Sunday comics come off

the press. I guess the only thing I really ever wanted to be was a cartoonist. And now, when I look back to those early days, I think the fellow who influenced me the most was Roy Crane who was doing *Wash Tubbs* and *Captain Easy.*

"I really liked the things that he did, and I wanted to do something of that kind myself for a long time. Later, George Herriman's *Krazy Kat* had a great influence on me, as did, of course, Al Capp and Milt Caniff. And I particularly enjoyed *Out Our Way . . .*

a great panel. *Popeye* was a great favorite of mine. Although there seems to be no comparison on the surface, in many ways my comic strip is like *Popeye* . . . if you're able to break through the surface to see it. Many of the things that happen in Charlie Brown are outrageous, and likewise many outrageous things happened in *Popeye*. I think *Popeye* was a perfect comic strip, consistent in drawing and humor.

"It's funny, but I never started out to do a cartoon about kids. I just wanted to be a good cartoonist like Herriman and Crane.

"Anyway, we finally got the comic strip sold in 1950, and the syndicate named it *Peanuts*. I was very upset with the title . . . and still am.

"The strip certainly was not an overnight success. It took a long time to develop—almost five years.

"Looking back on some of those early strips, you can see how radically the drawings have changed. But after this period of searching and experimenting, I started to bring in some new ideas . . .

"When I first started Charlie Brown, I didn't know he was going to lose all the time. He certainly wasn't the victim he is now. When he began, he had a personality a lot like Linus. He was slightly flippant . . . a kind of bouncy little character. He was able to come back with a wise saying to the other characters.

"When the strip first began, it had Patty, Shermy, Snoopy, and Charlie Brown. They were the only characters. Patty and Shermy were obviously going to be straight men. So this gave all the funny lines to Charlie Brown.

"When Lucy came into the strip, around the second year, she didn't do much at first. She came in as a cute little girl and at first she was patterned after our own first daughter. She said a lot of cute, tiny kid things, but I grew out of that whole 'tiny' world quickly and that's when the strip started to catch on . . .

"As Charlie Brown got more defensive . . . as Snoopy started to emerge as a different kind of dog . . . as Lucy started to develop her own strong personality, I realized I was really on to something different. And I think the security blanket really was *the* major breakthrough . . . suddenly these kids were being identified with many kids around the country. And then Snoopy climbed on top of the doghouse . . . and then this whole thing with Schroeder and Beethoven began. Charlie Brown actually was the first one to whistle some notes from the Ninth Symphony because I thought it would be funny to have this little kid whistling those complicated notes. Schroeder was only a baby at the time, but then I wanted to continue with the notes, and I thought of the toy piano, and baby Schroeder grew up very quickly thereafter. In fact, the next twenty years saw a basic evolution of the strip."

1950

1951

1952

1954

1955

1958

PEANUTS LOOK, IT'S A PICTURE OF SALLY, CHARLIE BROWN'S NEW BABY SISTER..

OH, ISN'T SHE CUTE? SHE'S REAL CUTE THAT'S SUCH A CUTE PICTURE

SHE SURE IS CUTE, CHARLIE BROWN SHE'S REAL CUTE YES, SHE'S REAL CUTE

IF THEY EVER TOOK "CUTE" OUT OF THE ENGLISH LANGUAGE, WE'D ALL PERISH!

PEANUTS THAT'S NOT A REAL BABY! THAT'S JUST A DOG DRESSED UP LIKE A BABY!

GOO!

PEANUTS LOOK, THIS IS **YOUR** BABY, NOT MINE! I HAVE MY OWN BABY SISTER AT HOME!

YOU WERE THE ONE WHO PUT THE BONNET ON HIM... NOW **YOU** TAKE CARE OF HIM!

I'M NOT INTERESTED ANY MORE.. I HAVE OTHER THINGS TO DO!

YOU'RE A POOR EXCUSE FOR A MOTHER!!

MAMA!

PEANUTS HERE, SNOOPY, LET ME TAKE THAT STUPID BONNET OFF YOUR HEAD..

THERE!

BOY, I'M GLAD THAT SILLY BUSINESS IS OVER..

I WASN'T SURE WHETHER I WAS GOING TO END UP IN AN ORPHANAGE OR AT THE HUMANE SOCIETY!

1962

PEANUTS 3-4

I THINK I'M LOSING MY FLAVOR!

PEANUTS

YOU BOUGHT A NEW KITE, CHARLIE BROWN? THAT'S CRUEL!

YOU'RE GOING TO TAKE THAT SWEET INNOCENT KITE OUT, AND TANGLE IT AROUND SOME TREE? OH, HOW CRUEL!

OR WORSE YET, YOU'RE GOING TO TANGLE IT UP IN SOME TELEPHONE WIRES WHERE IT WILL HANG ALL SUMMER, AND BE BUFFETED BY THE ELEMENTS! HOW CRUEL! OH, HOW INHUMANE!

I'D LIKE TO RETURN A KITE, PLEASE!

3-8

PEANUTS

YOU KNOW, LINUS, I ADMIT I CAN SEE SOME VALUE IN THIS BLANKET BUSINESS...

IT SEEMS TO PUT YOU IN A MOOD FOR CONTEMPLATION...I IMAGINE IT QUIETS YOUR MIND SO YOU CAN REALLY THINK ABOUT THINGS

ON THE CONTRARY..

I FIND THAT, TO BE DONE PROPERLY, SUCKING YOUR THUMB AND HOLDING YOUR BLANKET REQUIRES COMPLETE CONCENTRATION!

3-9

PEANUTS

HEY, MANAGER, WE HAVE AN IDEA TO IMPROVE THE OUTFIELD

IT'S TOO BARE OUT THERE...ALL YOU SEE IS GRASS...WHAT WE NEED IS SOME FLOWERS AND SHRUBBERY TO MAKE IT LOOK NICE

WE THOUGHT YOU'D WANT TO KNOW SO YOU COULD DO SOMETHING ABOUT IT...

I'M THE ONLY MANAGER WHO GETS A REPORT FROM A GARDEN COMMITTEE!

3-28

1964

PEANUTS 4-7

I DON'T **WANT** ANOTHER RABIES SHOT!

PEANUTS

WE'RE A COUPLE OF SORE-ARM BUDDIES, DID YOU EVER THINK OF THAT?

YOU HAD A RABIES SHOT, AND I'VE GOT 'LITTLE LEAGUER'S ELBOW'... THAT'S KIND OF FUNNY, ISN'T IT?

I GUESS IT ISN'T...

4-8

PEANUTS

"RABIES...AN INFECTIOUS VIRUS DISEASE OF THE CENTRAL NERVOUS SYSTEM IN DOGS"

YOU SHOULDN'T BE FUSSING ABOUT GETTING THAT SHOT... YOU SHOULD BE **GRATEFUL**!

WELL, IF YOU'RE **NOT** GRATEFUL, YOU **SHOULD** BE!!

THAT'S BETTER!

4-10

PEANUTS

YOU BOUGHT SNOOPY A PRESENT?

WELL, GETTING THAT RABIES SHOT WAS QUITE AN UPSETTING EXPERIENCE FOR HIM SO I THOUGHT A PRESENT MIGHT CHEER HIM UP...

BESIDES, IT'S SOMETHING HE'S ALWAYS WANTED...

4-11

PEANUTS

THIS KID AT SCHOOL SAID I HAVE A FUNNY FACE...

IS IT ALL RIGHT IF I TELL HIM YOU'RE GOING TO SLUG HIM? YOU CAN BE MY KNIGHT IN SHINING ARMOR...

I'D RATHER YOU DIDN'T

WHAT KIND OF A KNIGHT ARE YOU?

I'M A DOVE KNIGHT

PEANUTS

YOU STUPID KID, YOU THINK YOU'RE SO SMART!

I HAVE A BOY FRIEND WHO'S GOING TO CLOBBER YOU!

I'M NOT YOUR BOY FRIEND, AND I'M NOT GOING TO CLOBBER ANYBODY!

DON'T GO 'WAY! I HAVE TO TALK HIM INTO IT!!

PEANUTS

THIS KID AT SCHOOL INSULTED ME, SEE?

NOW, WHAT I WANT YOU TO DO IS BITE HIM ON THE LEG TO HELP ME GET EVEN WITH HIM..

BITE SOMEONE...JUST TO GET EVEN?

HOW GAUCHE!

PEANUTS

MY DAD LIKES TO HAVE ME COME DOWN TO THE BARBER SHOP, AND WAIT FOR HIM

NO MATTER HOW BUSY HE IS, EVEN IF THE SHOP IS FULL OF CUSTOMERS, HE ALWAYS STOPS TO SAY, "HI" TO ME...

I SIT HERE ON THE BENCH UNTIL SIX O'CLOCK, WHEN HE'S THROUGH, AND THEN WE RIDE HOME TOGETHER..

IT REALLY DOESN'T TAKE MUCH TO MAKE A DAD HAPPY...

Charlie's Travels

Charlie Brown, like most famous comic strips, is read around the world. Even before the moon shot, which made "Charlie Brown" and "Snoopy" famous throughout the world, *Peanuts* was being carried in newspapers in over sixty foreign countries.

Sometimes, of course, the comic strip suffers a bit in translation. In Finland, the name of the comic strip is *Tenavat*, which means "The Little Folks" . . .

In Italy it's *Pierino*, "Baby Peter" . . .

QUESTA È LA TUA MAZZA, CHARLIE BROWN? NON C'È SU IL TUO NOME...

DOVRESTI AVERCI SU IL NOME COME TUTTI I GRANDI CAMPIONI

LINUS HA UN INCISORE A FUOCO A CASA... VUOI CHE PRENDA LA TUA MAZZA E CI METTA SU IL TUO NOME?

CASPITA! SARÀ UNA COSA GRANDIOSA!

SARÒ L'UNICO DA QUESTE PARTI COL NOME SULLA MAZZA!

FARÀ UNA GRANDE IMPRESSIONE AI RAGAZZI DELLE ALTRE SQUADRE... AVRANNO PAURA A VEDERMI SCENDERE IN CAMPO... PENSERANNO CHE SONO UN CAMPIONE, E IO...

6-2

ECCO LA TUA MAZZA, CHARLIE BROWN!

HO AVUTO QUALCHE DIFFICOLTÀ CON L'INCISORE A FUOCO...

And in Sweden it's called *Snobben*,
which means "Snooty" . . .

In Holland, they say *Klein Grut*, or
"Small Fry" . . .

In South America, it's called
Rabanitos, "Little Radishes" . . .

And in Denmark, where there is no word for "peanut," the name is *Radiserne*, which also means "Radishes" . . .

The popularity of Charlie Brown overseas became evident when the Italian Communist Party decided to attack *Peanuts*, as reported by UPI:

ROME (UPI) — Charlie Brown may have good reason to look bewildered and exclaim "Good grief!"

He, his friends and the dog Snoopy who are in the Charles M. Schulz comic strip of "Peanuts" are either Fascists, have suicide complexes or are simply stupid, according to an Italian Communist party newspaper.

The first book of "Peanuts" has just been published in Italy. And since the Communist Party apparently has orders not to discuss the Russian-Chinese rift, it decided to throw its weight on other grave matters—like "Peanuts."

Titled "The Hysterical Friends of Charlie Brown," an article in the newspaper *Unita* said the comic strip is the product of "a society which revolves around the searching for individual success."

"The non-grownups of Charles M. Schulz are eight: Lucy, Linus, Schroeder, Patty, Violet, Pig Pen, the dog Snoopy and finally Charlie Brown," the newspaper said.

"All of the strips revolve around the personage of Charlie, the only one fairly normal . . .

"Lucy is before all the most hysterical. She is a hateful girl, a non-grownup and full of complexes, above all that of superiority. She is ignorant, but judges all and everybody, speaking continually of others . . .

"She believes she is the belly-button of the world, and therefore better than the others, thus able to resolve all problems. When one has turned the last page, you hate her. She is a Fascist. Patty, however, like Violet, is simply stupid.

"Linus and Schroeder, the two 'cases' more patent of the nervous group, have not elaborated their traumas, in which they are in up to their necks, and live in perpetual panic or in sublimation.

"Linus has a suicide complex. He saves himself by carrying a blanket which substitutes for the motherly breasts . . .

"Schroeder is taken by music, playing Bach, and getting mad when Lucy asks him what he will win if he is able to learn all the Beethoven sonatas.

"Pig Pen is a happy being, but only when he has covered himself with mud. If a bath takes off the dirt, he becomes agitated.

"For a psychic study, there is the dog Snoopy, which frequents their company. He also is hysterical. He varies between his own life as a dog and aspirations to become another beast or man. The depersonalization and the anguish carries him to imitate others.

"Thus, time by time, he imitates a rhinoceros or a lion or a kangaroo, or even Lucy or Patty. At the end he stretches out, taken with repentant sentiment and frustration.

"And Charlie Brown? He is the only one who is, precariously, at the middle road between mental health and nervousness.

"Faced with the strangeness of his friends, he remains overwhelmed or exclaims his alarmed 'Good grief' . . . full of a major apprehension for the well-being of humanity . . .

"In these funnies . . . it is not difficult to find a certain alienated America, always 12 years old, which does not know itself and does not realize it is the heir of a great history and a great culture: that America which yet has not discovered America."

What obviously had escaped *Unita*'s attention was that another left wing Rome newspaper, *Paese Sera*, has been running "Peanuts" for the last couple of years.

'I Am Not Now, Nor Have I Ever Been, a Member of the Fascist Party!'

Charlie and His Peers

And what do his fellow cartoonists think of Charles Schulz?

Each year, the National Cartoonist Society, composed of just about every major cartoonist in America, votes for the "outstanding cartoonist of the year." The winner is given the Reuben Award, designed by and named after the dean of American cartoonists, Rube Goldberg. The Reuben is equivalent to an "Oscar" or an "Emmy" in that the winner is selected by people within his industry.

Only one man has ever won the Reuben *twice* . . . his name, Charles Schulz.

REUBEN AWARD WINNERS

1946	Milton Caniff	*Steve Canyon*
1947	Al Capp	*Li'l Abner*
1948	Chic Young	*Blondie*
1949	Alex Raymond	*Rip Kirby*
1950	Roy Crane	*Buz Sawyer*
1951	Walt Kelly	*Pogo*
1952	Hank Ketcham	*Dennis The Menace*
1953	Mort Walker	*Beetle Bailey*
1954	Willard Mullin	*Sports*
1955	Charles Schulz	*Peanuts*
1956	Herbert L. Block	*HERBLOCK— Political Cartoons*
1957	Hal Foster	*Prince Valiant*
1958	Frank King	*Gasoline Alley*
1959	Chester Gould	*Dick Tracy*
1960	Ronald Searle	*Advertising & Illustration*
1961	Bill Mauldin	*Editorial Cartoons*
1962	Dik Browne	*Hi & Lois*
1963	Fred Lasswell	*Barney Google & Snuffy Smith*
1964	Charles Schulz	*Peanuts*
1965	Leonard Starr	*On Stage*
1966	Otto Soglow	*The Little King*
1967	Rube Goldberg	*Humor in Sculpture*
1968	Johnny Hart Pat Oliphant	*B.C. Political Cartoons*
1969	Walter Berndt	*Smitty*

3

A Studio Visit

CHARLIE SCHULZ works in this studio, designed by his wife Joyce, on the family's 28-acre ranch in northern California. Sparky works alone, except for his secretary Sue Issel, and he creates all the comic strips by himself, with no assistants. We asked Sparky to describe the creative process in the production of a Charlie Brown comic strip, with San Francisco photographer Tom Vano recording the sequence on film.

"I guess the question I am most frequently asked is 'Where do you get your ideas?' Of course, many of the original ideas came out of my own childhood . . . out of the dumb things I did when I was a kid . . . out of my own childhood loneliness. But you can only draw on your experiences for so much and then you have to start coming up with new ideas. Sometimes I'll just stare out my studio window for hours trying to come up with a good idea. As I told Barnaby Conrad one time, it's hard to convince people when you're just staring out of the window that you're doing your hardest work of the day. In fact, many times when I'm just sitting here thinking and therefore really working, I hear the door open and I quickly grab the pen and a piece of paper and start drawing something so that people won't think I'm just goofing off and anxious to have a little chat . . .

"But strangely enough most of my ideas come simply by sitting here at my drawing board and perhaps doodling around on this little pad of paper. I start off drawing what I hope will be funny little pictures of maybe Snoopy dancing or the kids arguing . . . or perhaps Linus is watching TV and Lucy comes in and turns it off and an argument starts. Sometimes I get something good right away and sometimes I sit here all afternoon and I can't think of a single thing . . .

"My equipment is extraordinarily simple . . . About all I need is four or five pens and a pencil. That doesn't give me very much for my income tax deductions. I use a soft pencil and about three types of pens. I use a C-5 Speedball pen for lettering, and a writing pen for most of the drawing. This has quite a strong point . . . it's one that will give you a fine line and also a very wide line if you want it. The Speedball pen comes in handy when I want Lucy to yell a big YOU, BLOCKHEAD! The Speedball pen I have now is only the second one I've used in my entire career . . . and I guess that's well over 20,000 drawings now. My first Speedball pen lasted for nearly 20 years. And then I use a small brush for inking in, say, Lucy's hair and some of the night scenes. That's about it, except for a ruler, a triangle, a drawing board, a bottle of ink, and of course the paper . . .

"Once I get an idea, I start to rough in the dialogue and pictures in pencil. I'm often asked why I don't have any assistants . . . to do the lettering or at least to ink in the letters. But that would be like Arnold Palmer having someone hit his chip shots. I like to do the lettering myself because I am constantly changing, constantly trying to improve what I have written down, and I continue to do this right through the inking stages of the words.

"I guess I'm a very competitive *person* and I always want the strip to be the very best possible. I still enjoy

drawing the comic strip as much now as I did when it first began. I still would rather draw a good comic strip than do anything else in the world. And I really believe that the word 'success' is relative. If I draw a good strip today, then I'm a success; if I don't, then I'm not.

"And it's still perfectly possible for me to sit here in this room all by myself with an idea which I think is really funny and to sit here and laugh at it while I'm drawing. And sometimes when I have what I think is a particularly good idea, I work myself up to such a nervous pitch that I can hardly letter the thing . . . I'm so anxious to get it down on paper . . .

"I try to do as little pencil sketching as possible, as I prefer to work directly with pen and ink. But the pencil stage involves the blocking of the characters. Good cartooning is basically good design. A cartoon character who looks good to you is a cartoon character who has been designed properly. You have to place things within these four panels so that you break the areas up into nice shapes. I have discovered that, because of the type of humor in Charlie Brown, the drawings must remain simple . . . very simple. And I rarely do any backgrounds. Keeping it all very simple is the key here.

"Eventually I get to the point where I can start inking in the characters. And once again I have to do it myself . . . I can't have someone else ink them in. Because this is really the art of the whole thing . . . getting the expressions just the way I want them. And I'm never quite sure just exactly what the expression will be until it comes right out of the end of the penpoint.

"I usually try to do an entire week, in other words six strips, at one time. It usually takes me at least an hour to complete a single strip. I have to keep six to eight weeks ahead and so I always have to be thinking what will be going on two months from when I'm drawing. A lot of people have written about the 'purpose' behind my comic strip—and I'm usually very flattered by these interpretations— but my chief purpose is to get the strips done in time to get down to the post office by five o'clock when it closes.

"Of course if all I had to do were the strips, I guess I wouldn't always be racing the deadlines. But I guess I spend as much time on the telephone as I do on the drawing board, so it's always pretty hectic. But we all have these different things going . . . the books . . . the dolls . . . the gifts . . . the TV shows . . . the new movie . . . the interviews . . . the requests. It goes on every day. But I enjoy most of these other things too. I enjoy being involved with them . . . and it makes me pleased to know that so many other people are apparently enjoying them. I feel as long as I continue to do the strip myself, as long as I try to improve upon or at least equal what I've been able to do, as long as all these other things don't basically hurt what I'm trying to do in the strip, then it's all okay . . . so I try to ration my time . . . but if I ever feel that the strip is starting to suffer, then some of these other things will have to go.

"After the six daily strips are completed, the Sunday page has to be done. This usually takes me a full day, since it involves not only three times as much work as a single strip but also color. In many papers across the country, Charlie Brown makes up the Sunday cover. I consider being on the front page a real responsibility and it's my duty to the editor and the reader to really give them something good, something special.

"Now I certainly don't call this great art. I've told a few interviewers that cartooning is a 'fairly' sort of a business. You have to be fairly intelligent—if you were really intelligent you'd be doing something else; you have to draw fairly well—if you drew really well you'd be a painter; you have to write fairly well—if you wrote really well you'd be writing books. So it's great for a fairly person like me. And it's what I enjoy doing most.

"I never want to disappoint all the people who read the strip. So it's

always like having a term paper to complete—every day—and the pressure is always there. I've learned that I can't please everyone all the time; but by trying to keep up on things, by reading as many of the latest magazines and new books as possible, I try to keep ahead of or at least up to what's going on in the world.

"As far as the drawing of the different characters, I guess I enjoy drawing Linus as much as any of the 'kids.' I like drawing his hair standing on end when Lucy has done something terrible to him; or the wide-eyed expressions on his face. Snoopy is really the easiest to draw. He's the most flexible—you can make his nose a little bigger or smaller without hurting anything. Charlie Brown is often a problem because that stupid round head is so difficult to draw, and, as you go around in that circle your hand always runs into the wet ink."

We asked Sparky which of his ideas has given him the most satisfaction:

"Well, I was always very pleased with the idea of the Great Pumpkin, which was a totally original thought. It started out where Linus was simply confused between Christmas and Halloween. It just popped into my mind one day and there it was . . .

"One of the best things that ever happened was the day that one of our teen-age boys, Monte, came up here to the studio. He was on a model-making kick of World War I airplanes, and he brought along one of the little plastic models he had been working on. He was standing there by the drawing board, and I hadn't been able to think of an idea all morning, and we started talking about the model he had made and about Baron Von Richthofen and other World War I things . . . and some of the old movies . . . and, anyway, he claims that he thought of it and I claim that I thought of it . . . but somehow we got Snoopy up there on the doghouse, and we put a helmet on Snoopy's head, and we had him start flying this crazy thing.   I hadn't even thought of the name Sopwith Camel at that time

but the whole thing took off!

"And of course all the ideas on how poor old Charlie Brown can lose give me great satisfaction . . . the kite . . . the little red-haired girl . . . the baseball games . . . the Valentines. But of course his reactions to all of this are equally important. He just keeps fighting back. He just keeps trying. And I guess that particular theme has caught the imagination of a lot of people nowadays; we all need the feeling that somebody really likes us. And I'm very proud that somehow all these ideas about Charlie Brown's struggle might help in some very small way . . .

"But perhaps the best idea I ever had, for me anyway, was Linus and the security blanket. I guess I would be most jealous of this idea if anyone ever tried to take it away from me. It suddenly made security blankets and thumb-sucking okay all around the world, and if we made parents a little less worried about their kids, then this would have to be one of my biggest thrills with the strip."

We asked Sparky if some ideas didn't pan out:

"Oh sure, many many times. I guess the best example is this: Many years ago I decided that it would be kind of funny, during the constant struggle that went on between Freida and Snoopy (she always wanted him to chase rabbits), if Freida were to bring in a cat in order to try to win out in some way over Snoopy. So I made up this cat Faron, after Faron Young the country western singer, but suddenly I discovered many things. In the first place, I discovered I couldn't draw a cat, which is a frightening thing to find out after you've already introduced a cat to the strip. And then I realized a very subtle thing was happening to the strip. And here we get right down to a basic analysis of humor. I discovered that by having a cat in the strip it was turning Snoopy too much towards being a real dog, and Snoopy in the comic strip is definitely not a real dog. He just doesn't act like a real dog. Snoopy acts and thinks like we animal-owners like to 'think'

our pets react in our wildest fantasies . . . but, no, he's not a real dog. But with the cat in the strip, Snoopy started to become more and more real, as he reacted to Faron like a real dog might react to a real cat. And it started to draw all the personality out of Snoopy. So the whole thing didn't work out and I think poor Faron is gone for good."

. . . And where does all this pressure lead to . . . ?

However, Sparky does take time to enjoy life . . . to pace himself from the demands and pressures of the daily strip.

Most of his spare time is devoted to his family (pictured here, left to right, his mother-in-law, Mrs. Dorothy Halverson, son Craig, daughter Meredith, son Monte, daughter Amy, wife Joyce, and daughter Jill, and one of the many family pets, Lucy). The photographs on these and the next two pages were taken by Bill Ray for *Life* Magazine's cover story on Charlie Brown . . .

The twenty-eight beautiful acres, set amongst California redwood trees, afford plenty of room for all types of family recreation, including paddle tennis, football, baseball, or just quiet walks . . .

But for the past year, Sparky's heart and much of his leisure time has turned to the Redwood Empire Ice Arena in nearby Santa Rosa, a family enterprise conceived, designed, and operated by Joyce Schulz.

It is considered by many experts to be the most beautiful ice arena in

the world and has held everything from concerts (Bill Cosby, Liberace, Rod McKuen), to ice-skating shows (Peggy Fleming skated at the opening), to skating classes.

And ice hockey buff Charles Schulz frequently will put on his John Ferguson shirt and hold family ice hockey matches with friends and neighbors.

Sparky even created a broom hockey league, with four teams involving over fifty local businessmen in one of the most rugged games on ice . . .

Facing off against Charlie Burns, coach of the Minnesota North Stars.

For many years, Sparky has enjoyed golf, especially participating in the Bing Crosby tournament. Here he sinks a birdie putt on the 16th of the Lucky Pro-Am tournament in San Francisco. His handicap has been a very low 4 and 5 and he usually shoots in the 70's.

Sparky and Joyce enjoy a Red Baron sequence.

4

You're in Show Business, Charlie Brown

The world's greatest baseball player, Willie Mays, meets the world's worst, Charlie Brown.

I guess it could be said that the person most responsible for my own association with the world's worst baseball player, Charlie Brown, was the world's best baseball player, Willie Mays.

In 1963 I was a struggling independent movie producer, having formed a small company with Sheldon Fay, Jr., a photographer-editor with whom I had worked at television station KPIX in San Francisco. We had located in Burlingame, seventeen miles down the peninsula—against all "expert" advice, for we were told we could never survive except in Hollywood or in New York. Nevertheless, having lived and worked in the Bay area, we decided we would rather fail there than succeed anywhere else.

For our first venture we decided to risk a few thousand dollars on a modest television documentary about Willie Mays. We were very fortunate: Ed Friendly, in charge of specials at NBC (he is now co-producer of *Laugh-in*), liked and bought the show, and when it was broadcast that fall, the ratings were good and the critics were kind.

But for the next six months, nothing happened. The calls we expected from networks, sponsors, and advertising agencies never materialized, and the money we had received from NBC dwindled away.

Then one day I was reading *Peanuts*, as I had been doing for over five years. And Charlie Brown was losing another ballgame, and Lucy came to the mound and shouted, "*Charlie Brown, you are the worst baseball player in the history of the world!*" For some reason, the image of Willie Mays and the cheering crowds came into my mind, as the antithesis of poor old Charlie Brown. And suddenly I thought, "Why not do a documentary on Schulz and *Peanuts*?"

I reached Sparky through a mutual friend, and it turned out that he had seen and liked the Mays show, plus some of the documentaries I had done at KPIX. He cordially invited me up to his studio. There he told me that many producers had approached him, either for a feature film or a television series, but that none of the offers had appealed to him. For example, one producer had suggested a "live" series, as had been done with *Dennis the Menace*; another had proposed three-dimensional animation like the old *Puppetoons*. Schulz, however, was concerned about "jumping in too quickly," especially with animation, since up to that time the only dramatizations of his material had been a few short TV commercials for Ford.

When I suggested that the best approach might be a documentary about his career, in which we could include some "pilot" animated sequences, he agreed to take the gamble. It is typical of him to have taken a chance on a guy from Burlingame after the biggest producers in Hollywood had been after him for years.

So for the next five months, we filmed every aspect of the world of Charlie Brown and Charlie Schulz. The animated sequences were created by an old friend of Sparky's named Bill Melendez, who had done the Ford spots. Like the Mays show, the whole production was done on speculation, as no network or agency would finance it. We figured, however, that this would be the easiest thing in the world to sell, and we borrowed heavily to complete it.

But then strange things started to happen, as they always do with poor old Charlie Brown. We took the finished hour special to the advertising agency for Ford, which had first option on it. The agency personnel raved over it, but Ford decided it wouldn't draw a big enough audience. We took it to Ed Friendly at NBC, who liked it but couldn't get NBC to buy it. We took it to the other two networks and to twenty top advertising agencies, and the answer was always the same . . . no! Those who actually saw it liked it, but no one would buy it. Some said we couldn't translate the success of the strip to television; others thought it was too innocent and slow-moving for the television audience.

A whole year passed, and no one was interested. As our loan at the bank came due, and as the whole project appeared to be heading for a typical Charlie Brown disaster, the Great Pumpkin—or Somebody—stepped in. In May of 1965 we received a phone call from John Allen of the McCann-Erickson agency, who had been enthusiastic about our show from the time he had seen it some nine months before. He said, "Our client Coca-Cola is looking for a special. By any chance do you have a format for an animated *Peanuts* show that could be connected with Christmas?"

"Absolutely," I replied, although of course I didn't have such a format. I figured we could certainly put something together in a month or so.

"Fine," he said. "Today's Friday, and we're meeting on Monday to settle our schedule for the year. Just airmail your outline to us in Atlanta, and we'll present it."

I gulped, in the true tradition of the funnies. "Something wrong?" he asked.

"No . . . no . . . fine . . . swell . . . great. . . . We'll have it there. Thanks a lot," and I hung up.

Next I called Sparky and explained that we needed a Christmas idea in about thirty minutes. In his calm, confident way he said that Christmas had always been one of his favorite themes and that he believed that we could do a meaningful Christmas special. So over the next day we worked out a rough format over the phone. It would have to be called

extremely rough, for it barely made one typewritten page, triple spaced.

I mailed the format to Atlanta late Saturday, and on Monday John Allen called. He asked, respectfully if disbelievingly, "Is this *it*?"

"That's *it*!" I shouted, feigning confidence, yet feeling like Charlie Brown on the mound. "Isn't it *great*?"

He paused and said, "Well, I'll add a few things and we'll see what happens. Wish me luck."

I didn't leave the phone for the next seven hours. But the phone call never came. I went home utterly dejected.

Next morning a telegram arrived at the office, and I guess it was the most exciting message we had ever received:

CONFIRM SALE OF CHARLIE BROWN FOR CHRISTMAS TO COCA-COLA FOR DECEMBER BROADCAST AT YOUR TERMS WITH OPTION ON SECOND SHOW FOR NEXT SPRING. GOOD GRIEF!

JOHN ALLEN

It was a thrilling moment: a sponsor had finally decided to gamble on the world's greatest loser, Charlie Brown, and our year-long fight had ended.

There is always tremendous responsibility and pressure involved in producing a television special. There is a heavy responsibility to the advertising agency and sponsor, who are risking several hundred thousand dollars in production time and air costs for a single program. And with this particular special we felt two additional responsibilities: to the fans and to the creator of the comic strip itself.

As soon as it was announced that we were going to do a Charlie Brown program, we heard from Charlie Brown's fans by letter and by phone. Many folks were cordial and wished us well, but just as many were quite concerned. As one young mother said, "These characters are so important to my kids. Please don't ruin them." And a caller from Palo Alto threatened to come down and punch me if we "wrecked the strip like movies and TV have wrecked so many things."

Some of the old doubts started to creep in: Since everybody had his own idea how the kids should sound, what voices should we select? Could we truly capture the mood of the strip in an extended, animated narrative? And we worried, too, about our responsibility to Sparky. This whole production was, ultimately, his "baby"; he was risking and entrusting to us the most popular comic strip in the world.

Thus we entered production with a sense of both excitement and concern.

Sparky had always said that the only person who could animate his characters was Bill Melendez, so we made a joint-venture agreement with Melendez and with Sparky, through his syndicate, United Feature. By now it was August, and we had only a short time to complete the show before December. I strongly recommended that we produce only a half-hour special, not only because of the short time available to finish the show, but also because I believed that the story could be a lot tighter and more effective. Bill, Sparky, John Allen, and Coca-Cola agreed, but CBS was at first doubtful. There had never been such a short entertainment special; they were worried that newspapers and magazines wouldn't promote it, and that the public would be disappointed. We insisted that if we produced a good show, no one would care how long it ran. Finally the network agreed.

Sparky, Bill, and I made some other basic decisions that were somewhat innovative at the time. We agreed to use, for the most part, the voices of real children—aged six to nine— rather than adults pretending to be children. And with the exception of Charlie Brown and Linus, we decided to use amateurs with absolutely no professional experience. Consequently, most of our "actors" came from our neighborhood in Burlingame. Since many of them couldn't read a script properly, and since some of the younger ones couldn't read at all, Bill had to feed them one line at a time during recording sessions. Often, when the words were fairly long, Bill had to break each word into smaller parts so the younger children could record them by syllables.

We all decided that the usual musical background for animation was

When Charles Schulz and Bill Melendez agreed to pose for some magazine pictures in front of Melendez's Hollywood studios, Sparky agreed to hold the ball . . .

. . . but he pulled a "Lucy" on Melendez at the last moment . . . You can never trust those cartoonists.

trite, so we tried jazz as a new approach. I asked jazz critic Ralph Gleason at the *San Francisco Chronicle* to name a musician who had kids and who read "Peanuts," and he answered, "Vince Guaraldi." Thus

Vince became musical director for the show. (John Scott Trotter would join us later as arranger and conductor for succeeding specials.)

Sparky and I had only one disagreement throughout production.

It was a result of my suggesting that we have a laugh track for the show. Sparky looked at me in horror, and said simply, "You must be out of your mind." I maintained that all comedy shows used laugh tracks, and he replied, "Well, this one won't. Let the people at home enjoy the show at their own speed, in their own way." There was no laugh track.

When Sparky completed the script, he proudly announced there would be one whole minute of Linus reading from the Bible. "But this is an entertainment show, Sparky," I offered gingerly. He just smiled, patted me on the head, and left the room.

Bill Melendez had to rush through the animation—he completed over 30,000 "cells" in less than three months, each cell needing to be inked and painted separately (as will be described later). Bill, like most animators, had served his apprenticeship learning the elaborate animation techniques of the Walt Disney Studios, but Bill agreed with Sparky that the style should be faithful to the strip. Consequently, the drawing was to be kept very simple —nothing fancy or "cartoony."

Bill finished the first "answer print" just a week before the broadcast date. We rushed it to the agency and to the sponsor who had taken the half-million-dollar gamble. They were quite pleased, but when we showed the film to two top CBS vice-presidents, neither of them laughed once. They didn't try to hide their disappointment. "Too slow . . . the kids don't sound pro . . . the music is all wrong . . . the story kind of wanders . . . the Bible thing scares us . . . the script is too innocent . . . but you gave it a good try, kid. . . ."

For a few hours, I felt lower than Charlie Brown's batting average. Quite frankly, I wandered around the streets of New York in a daze. But finally I was consoled by the memory of my own initial reaction to the show— that Sparky and Bill had created something extraordinary. I was able to forget those vice-presidents then, and to wait patiently until the votes came in—from the critics and viewers.

A Charlie Brown Christmas was broadcast December 9, 1965. John Allen summed up the reaction next day: "All heaven broke loose." According to the ratings, almost half of all the sets turned on that evening were tuned to Charlie Brown. The show received excellent reviews, and thousands of appreciative letters were sent to CBS, to Coca-Cola, and to Charles Schulz. Four months later the Peabody Award was given to the show as the "outstanding children's and youths' program for the year 1965," with the following citation:

Gentleness is a quality that is seldom understood by television writers and directors. A notable exception was . . . a little gem of a show that faithfully and sensitively introduced to television the "Peanuts" collection of newsprint characters created by Charles Schulz. *A Charlie Brown Christmas* was a delight for the whole family.

Producer Lee Mendelson (left) and director Bill Melendez (right) accept, with Charles Schulz, the Emmy Award for A Charlie Brown Christmas.

Five weeks after that Sparky, Bill, and I went to our first Emmy Award dinner, our show having been nominated as the best children's program of the year. We faced stiff competition, against Walt Disney, *Captain Kangaroo*, and an excellent *Stuart Little* special. Bill and I sincerely believed that we didn't have a chance. But when Kukla, Fran, and Ollie read the list of nominations, I think my heart stopped beating. And when they announced, "In Hollywood, the winner is *A Charlie Brown Christmas*," it was an overwhelming thrill.

Over the next five years we produced five other specials: *Charlie Brown's All-stars*; *It's the Great Pumpkin, Charlie Brown*; *You're in Love, Charlie Brown*; *He's Your Dog, Charlie Brown*; and *It Was a Short Summer, Charlie Brown*. According to the ratings, the eighteen broadcasts (including several repeats) averaged a share of the audience of 47 per cent, with an estimated 40 million viewers per show.

We plan to produce one new special a year, believing that a weekly series would not be good for us, for the viewers, or, most important, for Charlie Brown.

And what about the original documentary about Charles Schulz that nobody wanted? Four years later, in 1969, we updated it, Coca-Cola sponsored it, and it was broadcast by CBS. It was seen by 35 million people.

It may take Charlie Brown a long while, but he does win a few, now and then.

Charlie Brown's TV Credits

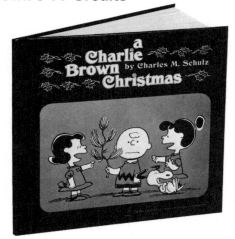

Originally broadcast on
December 9, 1965

Originally broadcast on
June 12, 1967

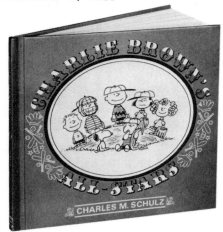

Originally broadcast on
June 8, 1966

Originally broadcast on
February 14, 1968

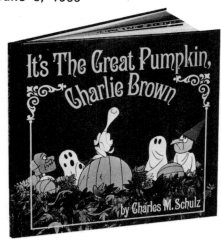

Originally broadcast on
October 27, 1966

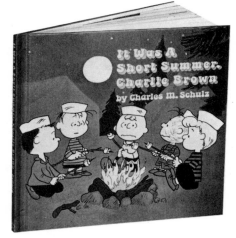

Originally broadcast on
September 27, 1969

Charlie Brown on Stage

And now that I've told you how smart I was to get Charlie Brown on television, let me relate how dumb I was in *not* getting Charlie Brown on the stage.

In 1966 Sparky told me of a young composer named Clark Gesner, who had written some songs about Charlie Brown. Sparky was quite taken by the music, so I agreed to listen to a demonstration record made by Gesner. The tunes were pleasant, I thought, but I could not share Sparky's enthusiasm, and, for my part, the subject was dropped.

A few months later, when I was visiting the Schulzes at their ranch, Sparky brought out another record. It seemed that Gesner had convinced a record company to put out an album of his songs, starring Orson Bean.

A few months later, Sparky called to tell me that Gesner had arranged to produce a stage show based on Gesner's music. I was quite surprised. "You mean a stage show with little kids singing and playing the parts? I don't think it can be done."

"No," Sparky replied. "They're going to use young adults, in their late teens and early twenties."

I really couldn't comprehend this. "Adults?" I said. "Seriously?"

He laughed, "You sound like the people who used to tell you we couldn't animate the strip."

"What do *you* think?" I asked him.

"Well, I think he's got a good idea. I love the music, and I think people with a little imagination can believe it. But most important, there's not a darn thing, they tell me, on the New York stage that a whole family can go and see nowadays. Wouldn't it be great if we could put on something that the whole family could enjoy?"

I recently spoke to Clark Gesner in his Brooklyn home to get his recollection of what happened. He said:

"I had made the demo record with Barbara Minkus, to play for Mr. Schulz, and he liked it. But for the next two years I couldn't get any record company to go for it. I went to a half-dozen or so, and they all turned me down. Another demo record was made, however—done by Barbara Minkus, Bill Hinnant, and me—of the second set of five songs which I had written in the meantime. Finally, a friend and fellow songwriter, Ruth Roberts, took the records to an old college classmate of hers, Mort Nasiter, who was president of MGM records. He liked it and said they would do it

"So Barbara, Bill, and I were joined by Orson Bean, and the album was made. Frankly, the record didn't do very well, and I think the fact that they put it out on a children's label hurt us. But I was quite confident that we had something special here. Oddly enough, what worried me was that some Broadway producer was going to ask me to make a show from the album. I really didn't want to do a record and have it end there, but I was frightened that a Broadway play—putting the *Peanuts* characters on stage—might somehow hurt the characters or the strip.

"Barbara Minkus, knowing my concern, knew a young producer named Arthur Whitelaw. She believed Arthur would do the job properly. I finally agreed to talk with him. But when he swept me off to Sardi's, all my fears started to come back. We had a wonderful initial discussion, though, and for the first time I saw that a stage show *might* be possible.

"Arthur told me he had thought of a *Peanuts* show ever since his high school days, and frankly I was caught up in his enthusiasm. We agreed that any show should be kept very simple —like the strip—and that it should be produced off-Broadway in a very small theater, not to exceed 300 people. It should have a small cast, simple costuming, a very small orchestra. It was going to be a "different" sort of musical, certainly, not for the sake of being different but just because that's what the subject required.

"A few days later I began to try to put some of the strips and ideas together to form scenes. I checked with Mr. Schulz to see if he agreed, and he said 'Go ahead.' So by the middle of December I found myself committed to the project in earnest,

holed up in Arthur's apartment, trying to make something theatrical out of the whole thing."

When Barbara Minkus had brought over the record she had done with Gesner, Arthur Whitelaw recalls, he listened to half of one tune (*Little Known Facts*), and insisted upon meeting Gesner immediately. Says Arthur: "Clark at first said 'no,' but the more we talked, the more he seemed to like the idea. Next, I played the record for Howard Otway, who owned a new 300-seat theatre called Theatre 80 St. Marks— it had just the intimacy we were looking for. Howard said, after hearing one song, 'The theatre is yours. And something else—if it doesn't do too well at first, I'll lower the rent to help keep it going. This should be great for the entire family.' I asked Clark when his record was going to be released, and he said in about a week. So we quickly ran over to MGM records and explained to Mort Nasiter that our show would be an excellent way to promote the record. Mort asked what the show would cost to get started, and I told him $16,000. We told him if he would put up half the money, we would put up the other half; he agreed on the spot and said we would have a check in the morning. Now *we* had to raise $8,000. I called a good friend of mine, Gene Persson, to see if he would co-produce the show and help finance it; he listened to the record and immediately joined the group. Things were really moving quickly. We decided to shoot for an opening either on March 7, my birthday, or March 27, Clark's.

"So while Clark started working on a book, Gene and I started giving auditions to nearly two hundred young actors and singers. Only one role was sewed up ahead of time; we knew Bill Hinnant, who had done the record with Clark, would be Snoopy. And then we hired Joe Hardy to direct. We started rehearsals January 13 and believe it or not we opened six weeks later—on my birthday, March 7."

I asked both Clark and Arthur if they thought, before the opening night, that they might have a hit. They both said they were confident that they had a good show, but they certainly didn't expect what actually followed.

As the curtain came down on opening night, both Arthur and Clark remember that there was good applause and great enthusiasm from everyone there. They couldn't put much faith in this reaction, however, since about 270 of the 299 people in the theatre were friends and relatives. "We went to a restaurant to await the results," Clark recalls. "The first review came on one of the television networks and it was so-so—the critic was pleased but certainly not overwhelmed—and a slight chill came across the room. One of the press agents said, 'Well at least we got one good quote we can use,' and

all my fears started to come back. But then the rave review from Walter Kerr in the *Times* arrived, and I realized all our lives would be changed forever."

And now let me tell you the record of that stage play that I thought wouldn't last a week. It cost less than $16,000 to produce, and it will probably gross well over ten million dollars in its first six years. It has been a smash hit in seven other cities in the United States and in half a dozen countries overseas.

I have now seen the show three times—in New York, in San Francisco, and in Los Angeles—and I must admit it is one of the most pleasant ways to spend an evening I have ever known. As Sparky predicted, children and adults alike share the enthusiasm. The words and music by Clark are delightful (I knew it all the time), and Arthur and Gene put together an unbelievably effective production: a tiny "orchestra"; a set made up of five pieces of wood in various shapes; costumes off the racks at Macy's; and a day in the life of Charlie Brown.

Gene recalls: "We called Sparky from New York after opening night to read him the Kerr review, and of course he and Joyce were delighted. He then asked very patiently, 'Now when do I get to see the script?' Arthur and I suddenly realized that we didn't even *have* a script. We had improvised from the various strips, with lead-ins to Clark's songs. So we

"FRESHLY DELIGHTFUL. A CONTINUOUS PLEASURE. FUN AND CHARM ABOUND."
—Richard Watts, Jr., N.Y. Post

"ONE OF THE GAYEST AND WISEST ENTERTAINMENTS IN TOWN."
—Emory Lewis, Cue Magazine

"A SMALL MIRACLE. EXPLOSIVELY FUNNY. UTTERLY WINNING."
—Walter Kerr, N.Y. Times

"A TOTAL DELIGHT"
— The New Yorker Magazine

"AN ENDEARING, IRRESISTIBLE ROMP"
—William Glover, Associated Press

GOOD GRIEF!

ARTHUR WHITELAW AND GENE PERSSON PRESENT

"YOU'RE A GOOD MAN CHARLIE BROWN"

A MUSICAL ENTERTAINMENT BASED ON THE COMIC STRIP "PEANUTS" BY CHARLES M. SCHULZ

MUSIC AND LYRICS BY CLARK GESNER

DIRECTED BY JOSEPH HARDY

ORIGINAL CAST ALBUM ON M-G-M RECORDS
MGM RECORDS ARE MANUFACTURED AND DISTRIBUTED IN CANADA BY QUALITY RECORDS, LTD.

had a girl take notes during the next three performances and rushed a script out to Sparky, who fortunately was very pleased."

These guys are nuts! The lowest budget in New York, a two-piece orchestra for a *musical*, and *no script*, and *no set*!!!

You're A Good Man, Clark . . . and Arthur . . . and Gene . . . but take it from me, you'll never get it off the ground.

The original New York cast of You're a Good Man, Charlie Brown: *Reva Rose,
Bob Balaban, Gary Burghoff, Bill Hinnant, Karen Johnson, Skip Hinnant.*

Drama Critics' Voting, 1967

	First Choice Play (3 pts.)	Second Choice Play (2 pts.)	Third Choice Play (1 pt.)	First Choice Musical (3 pts.)	Second Choice Musical (2 pts.)	Third Choice Musical (1 pt.)
WHITNEY BOLTON *Morning Telegraph*	Water			Cabaret		
JOHN CHAPMAN *Daily News*	Balance	Comedy	Water	Apple Tree	I Do! I Do!	Cabaret
HAROLD CLURMAN *Nation*	Homecoming			Abstain		
ETHEL COLBY *Jl. of Commerce*	Homecoming	Water	George	Cabaret	Apple Tree	I Do! I Do!
RICHARD COOKE *Wall St. Journal*	Homecoming			Cabaret		
JACK GAVER *U.P.I.*	Water	Comedy	Deer Park	Cabaret	I Do! I Do!	Apple Tree
RICHARD GILMAN *Newsweek*	Homecoming			Abstain		
WILLIAM H. GLOVER *A.P.*	Balance	Homecoming	Water	I Do! I Do!	Charlie Brown	
MARTIN GOTTFRIED *Women's Wear Daily*	Homecoming	Hurrah	World	I Do! I Do!	Dynamite	
HENRY HEWES. *Saturday Review*	Homecoming	Balance	Sweet Charlie	Annie	I Do! I Do!	Charlie Brown
TED KALEM *Time*	Homecoming	Hurrah	George	Abstain		
WALTER KERR *N.Y. Times*	Hurrah			Cabaret		
EMORY LEWIS *Cue*	Homecoming	Balance		Cabaret	Charlie Brown	Apple Tree
JOHN McCARTEN *New Yorker*	Abstain			Abstain		
HOBE MORRISON *Variety*	George			I Do! I Do!		
NORMAN NADEL *World Jl. Trib.*	Hurrah	Homecoming	Water	Cabaret	Apple Tree	Charlie Brown
GEORGE OPPENHEIMER *Newsday*	Balance	Homecoming	Water	Charlie Brown	I Do! I Do!	Apple Tree
WILLIAM RAIDY *Newhouse Papers*	Balance	Hurrah	Water	Cabaret	Charlie Brown	Apple Tree
RICHARD WATTS, JR. *Post*	Balance	Homecoming	Water	Cabaret	Charlie Brown	I Do! I Do!

Totals: Best Play, *The Homecoming*, 32 points; *A Delicate Balance*, 19; *You Know I Can't Hear You When the Water's Running*, 14; *America Hurrah*, 12; *The Killing of Sister George*, 5; *Black Comedy*, 4; *The Deer Park*, 1; *How's the World Treating You?*, 1; *My Sweet Charlie*, 1. Best Musical, *Cabaret*, 28; *I Do! I Do!*, 19; *You're a Good Man, Charlie Brown*, 13; *The Apple Tree*, 11; *Annie Get Your Gun*, 3; *Dynamite Tonight*, 2.

SR/June 10, 1967

Writer-composer Clark Gesner, producer Gene Persson, Mr. and Mrs. Charles Schulz, and producer Arthur Whitelaw at the opening night of the San Francisco production of the musical.

" YOU'RE A GOOD MAN, CHARLIE BROWN"

Charlie Brown tries to fly a kite in the San Francisco production of the musical. (Left to right: Al Perez; Janell Pulis; Wendell Burton; Austin O'Toole, kneeling; Roy Casstevens; Sydney Daniels.)

HAPPINESS

Happiness - 3

Happiness - 3

The original "Charlie Brown": Gary Burghoff.

A simple set for "Lucy," "Charlie Brown," and "Snoopy" atop his doghouse.

"Linus" (Joel Kimmell) frightens two of the girls as Count Dracula (girls: Rena Fredricks, Ann Gibbs) in the Boston production of the musical.

Rehearsal for the London opening of the musical.

Director Joseph Hardy (left) and producer Arthur Whitelaw in Stockholm for the opening night of the Swedish version of the musical.

Charlie Brown in the Movies

In addition to his great success on television and the stage, Charlie Brown also had a hit record. A rock group called the Royal Guardsmen recorded *Snoopy vs. the Red Baron*, and it sold close to three million copies.

Looking back now, I guess it was inevitable that Charlie Brown eventually would try to capture another goal in show business, namely a full-length feature film.

Back in 1965, when we still hadn't made a television sale, Sparky, Bill, and I had talked about a possible feature. We really didn't think we· were ready to go to ninety minutes, but it seemed that television was going to pass us by. But after a preliminary survey of the top motion-picture distributors, we discovered no one was interested in *Charlie Brown*—at any price. We were given many reasons: *Charlie Brown* had never been animated for over a minute; animation never did well overseas; only Disney could make money on an animated film; and so on.

Two years later, in 1967, with *Charlie Brown* now a hit on stage and television, Sparky, Bill, and I again discussed a feature. I had mentioned to Sparky that it was becoming increasingly difficult to find any picture to which I could take my children, and he too had been complaining that the movies were becoming less and

less family-oriented. In the same way that he had hoped the stage play would be an innovative show for the entire family, he now believed that movie theatres could use some family entertainment. In addition, Bill now had three animated TV specials behind him, and we had all learned a lot about what animated well and what didn't. Also, the challenge of a feature film, plus the excitement of worldwide distribution, gave us added incentive. Finally, we would be able to develop the characters to a much greater extent than the short twenty-six minutes of a TV special allowed.

We were astounded to discover, however, that all the major film companies turned us down. One man, Gordon Stulberg at Columbia, was the only movie executive who showed interest, but his eastern directors said no.

It was like reliving a bad dream all over again, and we still heard the same reasons why an animated feature was a bad investment.

During a visit to CBS-TV in New York, I dropped off a handwritten note to Dr. Frank Stanton, president of CBS, stating that the new TV show was coming along well. I also asked him if he knew anyone who might be interested in a feature.

A few days later, I received a call from Jack Schneider, one of the CBS group presidents. He said that CBS itself might be interested in a Charlie Brown feature for their new

motion-picture division. After a few meetings, we made a deal. Coincidentally, Gordon Stulberg was later named president of Cinema Center Films (the CBS-owned motion-picture company), and was delighted to make the picture he had tried to sell to Columbia two years before.

So an afterthought on a brief hand-written note had broken the log-jam.

On December 11, 1969, *A Boy Named Charlie Brown* opened at the Radio City Music Hall in New York, the first animated feature to be shown there in over twenty years. The film broke every major record of the thirty-seven year history of the Music Hall, including the greatest

advance sale, the greatest single day, and the greatest single week. Fortunately, most of the major movie critics (such as those from *Look, Time, The New York Times, New York Daily News*, etc.) gave the picture excellent reviews.

A Boy Named Charlie Brown is now playing around the world, providing the family entertainment for which Schulz "risked" his characters on the big screen.

Of course the co-producer and director of animation for *A Boy Named Charlie Brown* was once again Bill Melendez. Following is Bill's description of how he animates Charlie Brown:

After Charles Schulz creates the basic format and basic dialogue for the film, Melendez and his associates create a storyboard—the scene-by-scene picture outline of the script.

Melendez and one of his associates, Ed Levitt, discuss the completed storyboard and plot the action which will evolve from each scene.

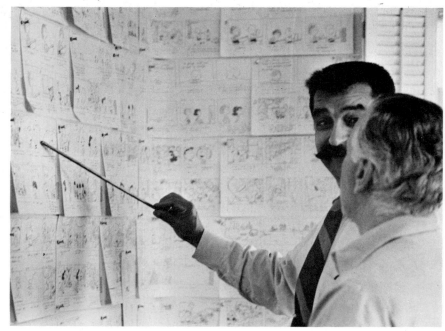

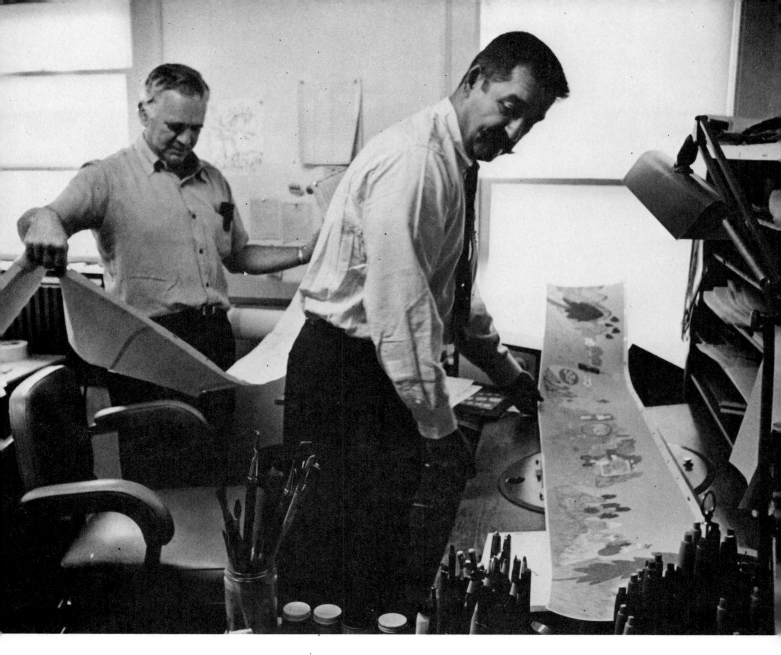

In "layout," drawings of the various settings are created, and the potential movement of the characters upon these settings is planned.

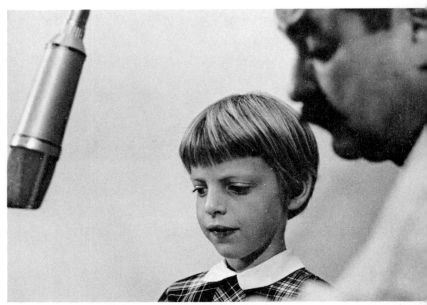

Below, Mendelson and Melendez discuss a scene from It Was a Short Summer, Charlie Brown. *Left to right are Gai DeFaria ("Peppermint Patty"), Linda Mendelson ("Freida"), Anne Altieri ("Patty"), and Sally Dryer ("Violet").*

Melendez directs the kids in yelling: "YOU'RE A BLOCKHEAD, CHARLIE BROWN!"

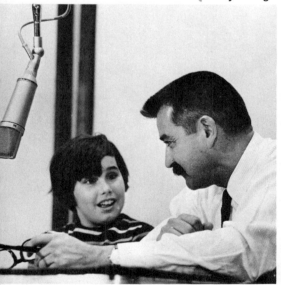

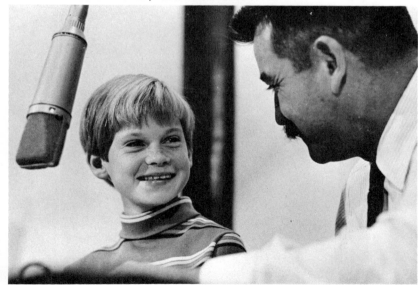

Each individual part must be recorded . . . often one line at a time. In the case of some of the younger children, who cannot read, it can be one word at a time . . .

Next comes the "reading" of the sound track. The editor measures the length of each spoken word of the dialogue. He breaks down the syllables into fractions of seconds, so that the animators can draw the proper mouth movements for the specific sound modulations.

The animators, draw the various phases of movement, a painstaking, exacting, time-consuming process.

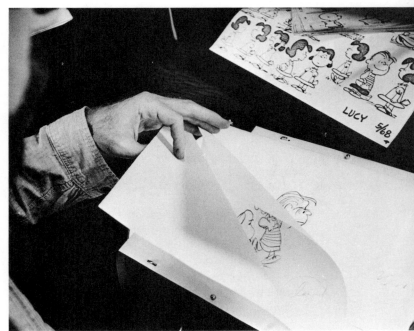

Each drawing by the animators changes just a fraction of an inch.

Eventually, there will be between 12 and 24 such drawings for each second of film.

The motion picture photographer films the "pencil tests" of the action . . . animation in its most basic form. Whereas motion picture film normally passes by the camera lens at 24 frames per second in constant motion, the photographer of animation clicks just one frame at a time. By changing the picture just slightly after each click, the characters start to "move."

The director then checks the "pencil tests" on a small viewing screen, called a "moviola," so that he can make any changes in action or expression before the final steps are completed.

The painters start to create the final backgrounds in color; and they also select the final colors for the characters, so that there will be an over-all harmony and blending of color.

The "scene checkers" must go through thousands of sketches to see that the arms, legs, hands, and heads are on the right bodies. There are many levels of "cells" for each action, and a character's head might be on one cell and his feet on another.

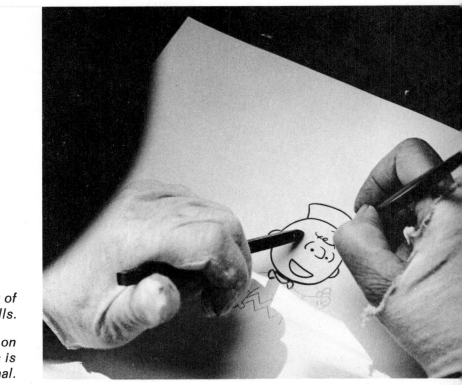

Inkers finish the outlining of the characters on the cells.

Again, the detail work on these thousands of cells is phenomenal.

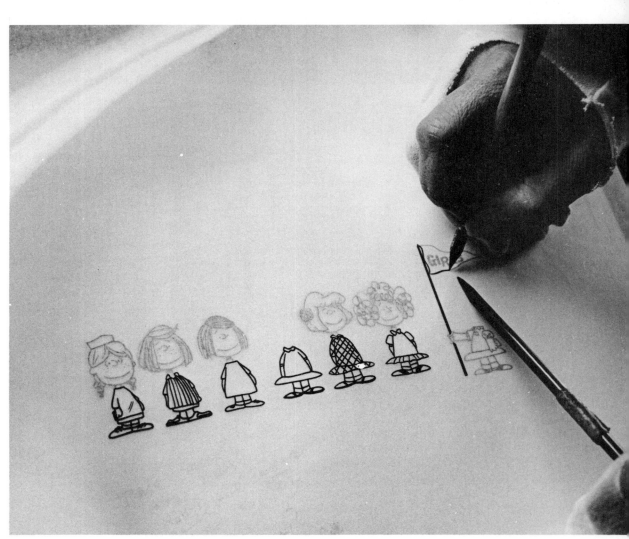

The quality of the pen line will determine the "believability" of the final animation.

Painters take each cell, flip it over, and start painting on the back side.

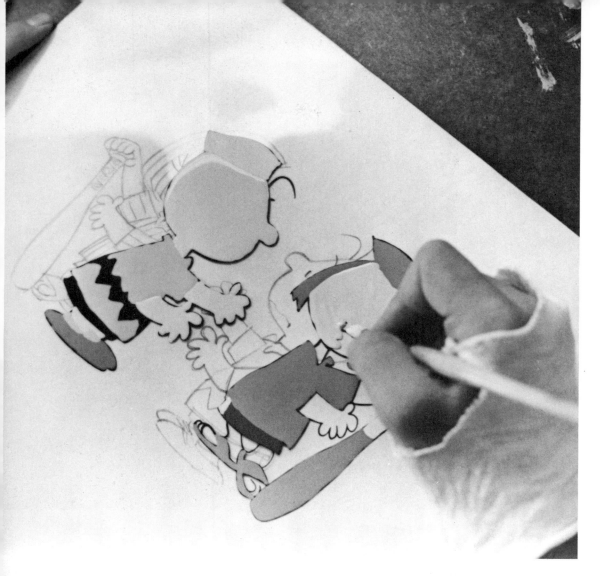

Each half-hour television special has more than 40,000 such cells, and the feature film has more than 200,000 cells. Each cell must be inked and painted to some degree.

The photographer then takes the painted backgrounds and the inked and painted characters, and he photographs one group of cells at a time, repeating the earlier process of the "pencil tests," only this time in much more detail, one frame at a time.

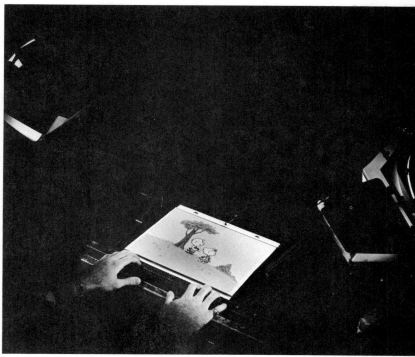

Meanwhile, the music has been written and performed by Vince Guaraldi and his orchestra, and arranged and conducted by John Scott Trotter. Rod McKuen joined Guaraldi and Trotter on the music for the feature.

Poet-composer-performer Rod McKuen, who wrote the words and music for the featured songs in the movie A Boy Named Charlie Brown, records the title song, which will then be animated.

The director and the editors (editors Bob Gillis and Chuck McCann seen here) now combine the various "tracks"—dialogue track, sound effects track, and music track—in a dubbing session at the recording studio, so that a composite single track is produced.

The editor and "negative cutter" match the combined track with the picture track, and the film is completed. It takes approximately eight months to produce a single Charlie Brown TV special, and approximately three years for a Charlie Brown feature.

Here are a few of the completed cells from the feature.

5

Snoopy— This is Houston Control

THE worldwide impact of Charlie Brown is of course quite evident in the phenomenal sales figures of Charlie Brown's hardback and paperback books. Sales have just passed the 55 million mark, certainly by far the greatest success ever enjoyed by a comic strip character or, for that matter, by any author in history.

Happiness Is a Warm Puppy, first published in 1963 by Connie Boucher's Determined Productions, topped both the adults' and children's best-seller lists and inspired national and international campaigns with the theme of "Happiness Is . . ."

The Gospel According to Peanuts, by Robert Short, has now passed the 2 million mark in sales, and Short's sequel, *Parables According to Peanuts*, is doing equally well.

And of the top fifty-eight paperbacks sold last year (those selling over 600,000 copies), sixteen were Charlie Brown editions.

Sparky writes two or three originals each year, of which *You're in Love, Charlie Brown*, based on the TV show, and the books on *Snoopy and the Red Baron* are among his favorites.

But this unprecedented record in publishing is not the only indication of the international success of *Peanuts*. Charlie Brown and his friends have appeared on more magazine covers than any other comic strip character in history.

Woman's Day 20¢

Prizewinning Storage Ideas
Valentines to Make
Help for Overweight Teens
Quick-change Artistry with Your Hair
Cook Book of European Potato Favorites
$$-Saving Menus • Fabulous Fricassees

PREVIEW OF THE NEW "PEANUTS" TV SPECIAL

Are You Overcharged for Auto Repairs?

SR's SEVENTEENTH ANNUAL ADVERTISING AWARDS

Saturday Review

April 12, 1969 50¢

PSYCHIATRIC HELP and MAGAZINES

THE DOCTOR IS VERY IN

The Not-So Peanuts World of Charles M. Schulz
(See Communications)

BIAFRA AND THE AMERICAN CONSCIENCE
by Senator Charles E. Goodell

THE VALUATOR

SPRING '69

IN THIS ISSUE
Interviews: "Peanuts" creator Charles Schulz, Myron Lieberman, critic of American Teacher Associations.
Special Report: "California's Drug Revolution" Part III
Plus . . . Guest editorials, book reviews, travel, entertainment, purchasing opportunities . . .

I AM A GREAT ADMIRER OF THE MODERN SCHOOL TEACHER!

Tm. Reg. U. S. Pat. Off.—All rights reserved
© 1969 by United Feature Syndicate, Inc.

JULY 1969 • 50c
U.S. CATHOLIC AND **Jubilee**

Peanuts the theologian

Is there any future for monasticism?

How the church looks to a black priest

'TEEN • Young America's Fashion, Beauty and Entertainment Magazine

'TEEN.

SEPTEMBER 35¢
1969 U.K. 3/6

**The Great 'TEEN Takeover
by the Peanuts Gang**

Charlie Brown,

Lucy, Linus, Snoopy & friends

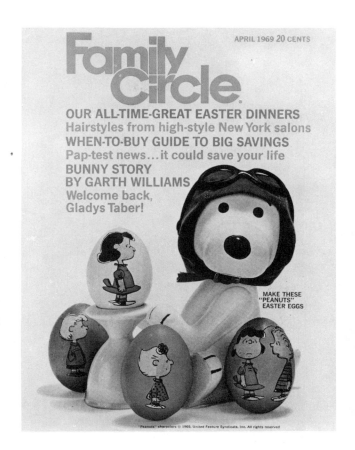

APRIL 1969 20 CENTS

Family Circle.

OUR ALL-TIME-GREAT EASTER DINNERS
Hairstyles from high-style New York salons
WHEN-TO-BUY GUIDE TO BIG SAVINGS
Pap-test news…it could save your life
**BUNNY STORY
BY GARTH WILLIAMS**
Welcome back,
Gladys Taber!

MAKE THESE
"PEANUTS"
EASTER EGGS

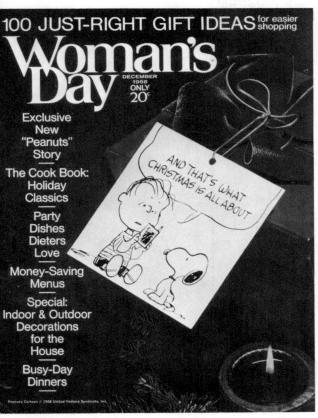

100 JUST-RIGHT GIFT IDEAS for easier shopping

Woman's Day

DECEMBER
1968
ONLY
20¢

**Exclusive
New
"Peanuts"
Story**

The Cook Book:
Holiday
Classics

Party
Dishes
Dieters
Love

**Money-Saving
Menus**

Special:
Indoor & Outdoor
Decorations
for the
House

Busy-Day
Dinners

AND THAT'S WHAT CHRISTMAS IS ALL ABOUT

SAN FRANCISCO

APRIL 1964 | 50¢

CANDLESTICK PARK

LMFP
Burlingame

SCHULZ

MAKING THE SCENE
AT CANDLESTICK

NEVER PLEAD
WEALTHY: PART II

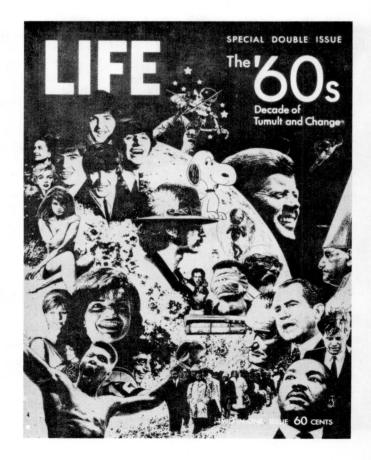

Security is an Eye Patch

STARRING SALLY AND CHARLIE BROWN

U.S. DEPARTMENT OF HEALTH, EDUCATION, AND WELFARE • Public Health Service

Charlie Brown and his friends have sparked various campaigns involving health, including booklets for the U.S. Department of Health, Education, and Welfare on eye care, and for measles vaccine (following page).

BLAST YOU,

RED MEASLES!

I'll Get You Now!

Measles Clinics

ARE COMING!
IN
JANUARY

HAPPINESS IS NO MORE MEASLES

And in the stained glass window of the Westminster Presbyterian Church in Buffalo, New York, such famous people as Bach, Martin Luther, Duke Ellington, and Dr. Albert Schweitzer are joined by Schroeder and his toy piano. Can you find him? He's in the lower left corner of the seventh panel in the left column.

Reports of the Great Pumpkin, not unlike UFO's, come in weekly from around the country; *Rapid City* (South Dakota) *Journal* photographer Ken Norgard recorded this one . . .

. . . and this one was reported by the
Northville Record-Novi News.

Good Grief, The Great Pumpkin!

The search for the Great Pumpkin by Charlie Brown, central figure in the popular Peanuts comic strip, may finally have come to a successful conclusion — right in our own backyard. Believe it or not, that's Charlie Brown above, happily perched inside our version of the Great Pumpkin (a 125-pound Northville grown giant). Our Charlie's the son of Ernest Brown, reporter for The Northville Record-Novi News. And if that's not enough similarity, consider the fact that Mrs. Brown's maiden name was Schultz, just a letter different than the cartoonist's own name, Charles Schulz. "It's the Great Pumpkin, Charlie Brown" will be shown tonight at 7:30 on Channel 2. See related story on Page 11-B.

Of course, Sparky receives clippings from readers all over the world, plus gifts for the characters. One lady in North Carolina hand-knit an entire winter outfit for Snoopy. After the TV special on Halloween, when Charlie Brown received only rocks in his trick-or-treat bag, a girl's college dormitory sent five boxes of candy for him. But the most exciting and interesting mail involves the hundreds of letters which come into Sparky's studio each week, such as these two:

6206 n. Washtenaw
Chicago 45, Ill.
Dec. 18, 1961

Dear Mr. Schulz,

In your December 17, 1961 "Peanuts" you made a couple of Errors! The passage you printed was not in its actual form. The original Hebrew of Jeremiah 31:15 is

כֹּה אָמַר יְהוָה קוֹל בְּרָמָה נִשְׁמָע (מְאֵן)
נְהִי בְּכִי תַמְרוּרִים, רָחֵל
מְבַכָּה עַל־בָּנֶיהָ מֵאֲנָה לְהִנָּחֵם
עַל בָּנֶיהָ כִּי אֵינֶנּוּ.

The literal translation is —

Thus said the Lord — I hear a voice in Ramah, lamentations and strong crying, Rachel is crying because of her sons and she didn't want to be comforted because they weren't.

I think you may receive other letters about certain mistakes

To Charlie Brown + Snoopy with love.

PEANUTS By Charles Schulz

545 Wolcott Ave.
Beacon, N. Y.
Feb. 24, 1967

Dear Mr. Schulz,

We realize that our "huge St. Bernard", Kaiser Wilhelm, has been on the loose at the local school playground almost every morning lately. After reading your comic strip in the Feb. 24 issue of the Beacon Evening News, we promise to take extra care to make certain Kaiser is secure in his pen before we leave for school in the mornings from now on in order that Snoopy won't be in danger of being "racked up."

We remain your loyal fans,

P. S.
Kaiser really
is a coward at heart.
We enclose his picture.

Chris and Kaiser
Sjoholm, and
Erik Sjoholm

137

Good Grief! Snoopy Makes Macy's Parade

Snoopy seems to get as much attention as his master, Charlie Brown. Here he becomes a Goodyear Blimp . . .

and winds up in the Macy's Parade . . .

. . . seamen have formed on the deck of an aircraft carrier to create Snoopy in silhouette . . .

. . . Bill Harper of Redding, California, even got Snoopy airborne . . .

. . . and John and James Miller of Racine, Wisconsin, created a snow Snoopy.

The Wall Street Journal reported Snoopy's participation in the Petaluma, California, Wrist-Wrestling Meet . . .

Snoopy Has Arrived And Petaluma Will Never Be the Same

* * *

But Dog Doesn't Stand Chance In Wrist - Wrestling Meet; Some Hazards of the Sport

By JAMES E. BYLIN
Staff Reporter of THE WALL STREET JOURNAL
PETALUMA, Calif.—Petaluma?

Yes, Peanuts fans, there really is a Petaluma. Snoopy arrived here yesterday, dinner bowl on his head but the globe that had guided him lost somewhere along the way. He had come, of course, for the world's wrist-wrestling championship. Yes, there really is a world's wrist-wrestling championship. It's scheduled for tonight, and, thanks to the lovable beagle from the Charles Schulz cartoon strip, it's a sellout.

"The town's going wild. It's jammed full of people, and the fever's up—like a big prize-fight in New York City," says William Soberanes, local wrist-wrestling impresario and columnist for the Petaluma Argus-Courier.

Until Snoopy started his odyssey, Petaluma, with 22,000 people and hundreds of thousands of chickens, was best known as "the egg basket of the world." But now all that has changed, according to Mrs. Helen Putnam, a grade-school principal who is Petaluma's mayor. Now, says the lady mayor, "All roads lead to Petaluma."

Actually, not many roads at all lead to Petaluma, which is about 30 miles north of San Francisco and 10 miles north of Novato. (Novato?) Interstate 101 has a Petaluma turnoff, but it's a couple miles outside of Petaluma, a fairly flat city whose Indian name means city of many hills.

Signs, but No Band

In yesterday's Peanuts strip, Snoopy arrived here after dark, and there was no one to meet him. "Rats. No band," he said forlornly. In fact, "Welcome Snoopy" signs dot the town, along with directions for the hiking beagle to find his way to the 2,500-seat Veterans Memorial Building, site of the matches. Once Petalumans knew the dog was coming, they went all out.

And well they should have. For Snoopy has put Petaluma on the map, if not on the globe. "The reaction from all over the country has been tremendous. We could draw 10,000 if we had the room," says Mr. Soberanes, who started the wrist-wrestling matches in the back room of a bar 15 years ago. "Maybe next year we'll go outdoors. We're in the town's biggest auditorium now."

If the truth be known, Snoopy's trek hasn't been quite as adventurous as the comic strip has made out. The dog's creator, Mr. Schulz, a friend of Mr. Soberanes, lives only 15 miles away, in Sebastopol. (Sebastopol?)

Not only that, here's another blow to Snoopy fans: The dog doesn't stand a chance in tonight's matches.

There are more than 100 wrist-wrestlers, from about 30 states, entered in tonight's matches, and some of them weigh more than 300 pounds. The average beagle weighs only 32½ pounds, though a beagle is a bit quicker on his feet than a 300-pound man.

Contestants compete standing up, which is another disadvantage for a Beagle. They place their elbows on a specially built table, using foam rubber pads to ensure that the wrists are at an even height. (If they weren't even, a man with a longer arm would have a leverage advantage.) The contestants then lock thumbs, the referee hollers "start" and the match is on. Each tries to push the other man's arm to the table. Most matches are over in a matter of seconds.

"In the movies, you see guys locked in combat for a half hour or so, but that's impossible," says Mr. Soberanes, who knows quite a bit about wrist-wrestling. "Five minutes is the ultimate. After that, you're through for the night."

The Hazards

The competition isn't without its hazards. A couple of years ago a lumberjack walked on stage and immediately fell off, into the audience. He had to be carried out. Another time a cowboy strained so hard he snapped his belt and his pants fell down.

There's a women's division here, too, and the women don't always behave like ladies. "One year this gal blew her top and tried to tear the referee apart," recalls Mr. Soberanes. "She charged the referee gave the other girl the event because she was prettier."

Being a top wrist-wrestler is not all fame and glory. "I keep getting calls in the middle of the night because someone has a guy they think can beat me," says James Pollock, a 195-pounder who won the light-heavyweight title here last year. He adds: "Half the time, I go."

Mr. Pollock says there is more than brawn to wrist-wrestling. He uses psychological warfare. Sometimes he tries to stare his opponents down. Other times, he snarls.

But there really is no substitute for weight. The defending champion in the unlimited class—where anybody can compete—is a 333-pound man from nearby Cotati.

Cotati?

In fact, people were starting to "see" Snoopy everywhere . . . from a speck magnified 700 times . . .

SNOOPY GETS AROUND—He sure does! But, of all places, you would never expect to find him in a spent HFIR fuel plate specimen. That's where he was found though by a trio of sharp-eyed metallographers during a routine examination. He was noticed first as an unusual speck, then magnified approximately 700 times and there he was. This particular Snoopy was formed by a reaction of fuel materials during irradiation. The dark area is U_3O_8, the background is aluminum, and the light gray area is a reaction product between the two. Al Richt, Ray Wallace and Earl Sims of Metals and Ceramics Division discovered the little fellow—apparently headed for his Sopwith-Camel!

. . . to perching on Joshua trees in Arizona . . .

World War I Flying Ace
Perched on Joshua Tree

TWENTYNINE PALMS — Snoopy clashed with the Red Baron in the skies over the Joshua Tree National Monument recently and thought he had downed the Baron, but it was a ruse and Snoopy found himself, luckily, perched on top of one of the Monument's Joshua Trees, looking for help and a way to get down.

The incident was said to have been reported to the information office at Twentynine Palms Marine Corps Base, and S. Sgt. Jack Holsomback went to the Monument and caught this photograph of Snoopy against the desert sunset. It being against regulations to touch or remove any part or living thing in the Monument area, Holsomback sadly left Snoopy on his own.

That, at least is Jack's story, and one easily verified by anyone finding the precise Joshua tree in the half-million acre expanse of the park.

ON GUARD — Snoopy comes a cropper in Joshua Tree National Monument and is pictured by Marine S. Sgt. Jack Holsomback as he seeks help.

... to the rim of the Grand Canyon ...

The Contemporary Canyon—
text, photograph by Don Dedera
Grand Canyon deserves and has grandiose
place names: Zoroaster Temple, Vista
Encantadora, Phantom Ranch, Hindu
Amphitheater, Shinum Altar.
But today, amidst the elegantly described,
there is a place nicknamed, "Snoopy Sleeping
on His Doghouse." "Snoopy Sleeping
on His Doghouse" is best seen
from the Kaibab Trail, but also is
visible from the Rim Drive east of Grand
Canyon Village and would be especially
astonishing to the Red Baron, should he be
flying down the canyon.

... and even Snoopy was starting to
see Snoopy everywhere ...

... so much so that a national
campaign for "Snoopy for President"
was launched ... causing enough
problems that the California
legislature passed a law to make it
illegal to write in a fictional character's
name on the ballot ... but Snoopy,
alas, lost anyway ...

144

Of course, Snoopy has been very proud to represent dozens of organizations around the world . . .

And then came the highest honor so far for Snoopy. The news release from NASA, Houston, on Wednesday, March 6, 1968, read: " 'Snoopy the Astronaut' has been recognized as the humorous symbol of good work by the NASA astronauts. Captain Alan Shepard, speaking for the astronaut team, has acknowledged Snoopy as the 'watchdog' of Apollo. His job will be to promote excellence in every phase of Apollo manufacturing and checkout and thereby assure crew safety and mission success.

"This emblem is awarded in recognition of individuals who demonstrate professional excellence in their daily efforts on the manned space flight program."

And then came the supreme honor, the highest tribute ever paid to a comic strip in history, or, for that matter, to *any* fictional character. We talked with Commander Thomas Stafford, of Apollo 10, about the event:

"Our Apollo 10 crew of course has the right to pick its own code names . . . after Apollo 9 had used 'Spider' and 'Gumdrop' as their code names, we didn't want to just call ours 'Spider 2,' so we started thinking of possible alternatives. And we thought 'Snoopy' would be perfect for the LEM, since we had selected Snoopy earlier in the year as NASA's overall emblem of excellence . . . so we thought by calling it 'Snoopy,' we would thus be honoring all the people who helped build the entire program. But we really didn't think about a name for the command module at first. Then one day —during a simulation—someone, I think it was John Young, said 'Good grief, Charlie Brown,' and we suddenly thought that 'Charlie Brown' would be a great partner

for Snoopy in space . . . and that's how it came about. And we got a big kick out of holding up the drawings of the characters in space . . . it all added some much-needed humor to a very intense mission . . ."

We have mentioned earlier that Charles Schulz is a gambler, a man who doesn't sit pat on success. *The New York Times* headlined: "Creator of Peanuts Tempts Fate on Apollo Mission." Certainly, if a tragedy had occurred, as well it might have, the symbols would forever remain in man's mind as symbols of disaster. But Sparky has always had faith in the Apollo program, from the very start, and he felt if those men could risk their lives, the least he could do would be to risk the popularity of the characters.

He said just before the launch of Apollo 10: "It's nice to be involved in a little way in something that's so beyond your comprehension. When

Thomas Stafford called me a few days ago and said our names had been chosen, it was a tremendous thrill for me, especially for an old Buck Rogers fan. To know your characters would be the first to really go to outer space is I guess the most exciting thing that ever happened to us."

And so they took off, for the closest look at the moon in history. I'm sure that all of us connected with Charlie Brown listened even more intently to the progress of Apollo 10. We were thrilled to see the astronauts hold up pictures Sparky had drawn as they raced to the moon. And then came that fateful point—on the far side of the moon—where the command module and LEM would separate, when "Charlie Brown" and "Snoopy" would separate and no one would know for many minutes if everything was going all right. I sat frozen by the television set. Nothing. Silence, as had been expected, but still terrifying. Still nothing. And then . . . "Charlie Brown" and "Snoopy" radioed back their historic "separation."

As "Snoopy" docked with command module "Charlie Brown," this picture was flashed on the Houston Manned Spacecraft Center screen.

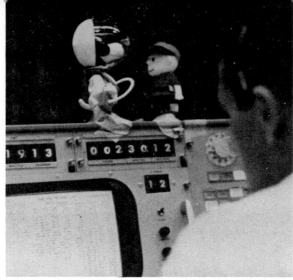

*Good luck charms on a monitor
at Houston control . . .*

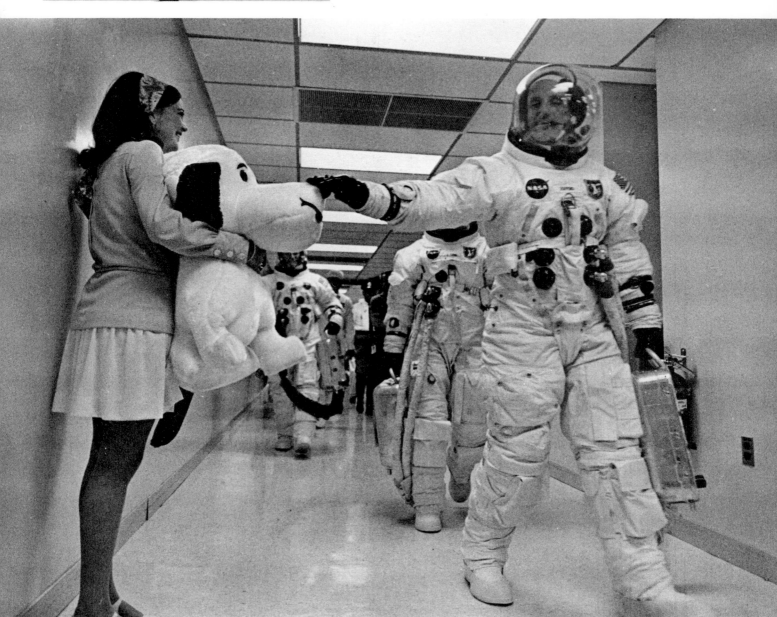

*Astronaut Thomas P. Stafford pats "Snoopy" as he and fellow astronauts Young and Cernan
start the pre-launch countdown.*

Back home safely, the crew of Apollo 10 meets Governor Ronald Reagan and Charles Schulz at ceremonies at the State Capitol in Sacramento, California . . .

The American Paper for Americans

Chicago Tribune
THE WORLD'S GREATEST NEWSPAPER

SPORTS **FINAL**
★★★★

84 PAGES, 4 SECTIONS   10c

122d YEAR—No. 143   © 1969 Chicago Tribune

FRIDAY, MAY 23, 1969

CHARLIE AND SNOOPY DOCK!

IL PROGRESSO
ITALO-AMERICANO

The First and Greatest
Italian Language Daily
in the USA and Canada
★ ★ ★ ★

Anno XC — N. 143   SECOND CLASS POSTAGE PAID AT N.Y., N.Y.   260 Audubon Ave., New York, N.Y. 10033 — Venerdi 23 Maggio 1969   TEL.: (212) 795-5500   10 Cents la Copia

RASSEGNA

A INDIANAPOLIS *brivido*
a Pag. 5 *per Andretti*

CANNES: *successo*
a Pag. 7 *di "Flashback"*

Atmosfera appesantita in Italia

Lo scontro frontale tra le due correnti opposte in seno al Comitato Centrale del Partito Socialista italiano non è avvenuto, e non per una azione risolutiva che eliminasse o appianasse il dissenso; lo scontro è stato soltanto rinviato, e così quella atmosfera di crisi che incombeva sulla vita politica italiana lungi dal diradarsi, si è appesantita. Sull'imbarazzante posizione di stallo in cui si trova la vita nazionale ogni recriminazione è inadeguata ai rischi ai quali rimane esposto il Paese, mentre sul tappeto sono urgenti e gravi problemi.

Il passaggio obbligato della crisi che investe anche il governo e la sua effettiva funzionalità non indurrebbe

DOPO LA MISSIONE VICINO ALLA LUNA

"Snoopy" ritrova
"Charlie Brown"

'SNOOPY' SAFE AFTER PERILOUS MOON TRIP

AT STANFORD

The American Paper for Americans

San Jose Mercury
1851-1969

Chicago Tribune
THE WORLD'S GREATEST NEWSPAPER

★★★★★★
FINAL

10 Cents

SPORTS **FINAL**
★★★★

122d YEAR—No. 147   © © 1969 Chicago Tribune

TUESDAY, MAY 27, 1969

64 PAGES, 4 SECTIONS   10c

NEXT: A MAN ON THE MOON

Apollo Return and Pickup Flawless

OGILVIE TAX, BUDGET PLAN FACES FIGHT

Chamber's Plea Gains Backing

BY GEORGE TAGGE
[Political Editor]

WE'RE BACK!

TRIO ABOARD SHIP IN ONLY 39 MINUTES

Hit Water 3 Miles from Carrier

NASA'S FOCUS FOR FUTURE IS MAN ON MARS

Lunar Trip Set

The Great Pumpkin

Zschiesche

GOOD MAN IN THE MOON

Of course the mission was a complete success and Apollo 10 paved the way for the most historic mission of all human existence, Apollo 11. And the whole world, if they didn't know about Charlie Brown beforehand, certainly knew about him now:

Oh, Good Grief! Red Baron Wins

HOUSTON (UPI) — Apollo 10's astronauts were congratulated Friday for doing something the Red Baron has been trying to do for years—they got rid of Snoopy.

The lunar module, nicknamed after Charles Schulz' comic strip dog Snoopy, was jettisoned Friday and headed toward sun orbit.

Ground communicator Jack Lousma told the Apollo 10 astronauts: "I've got a congratulatory message for you here. It says congratulations on doing what I've been trying to do for a long time. Signed, the Red Baron."

Snoopy for years has waged make-believe battles with his arch-enemy, the Red Baron. The real baron was Manfred von Richthofen, a German flying ace of World War I in 1914-18.

In Sebastopol, Cal., Charlie Brown's reaction to the flight of Snoopy around the moon was predictable.

"Good grief," mumbled Charlie Brown (through Schulz).

As for the floppy-eared Snoopy: "He told me he was well equipped for the trip, what with his great background as an authentic World War I flying ace," Schulz said.

When it was all over, we asked Sparky about his feelings during the flight. "Oh, I guess everybody always has fear about those kinds of things but I really thought it would come out all right."

And then he reminded me that over a year before Apollo 10, Snoopy had made his own journey to the moon, thus beating "the Americans, the Russians, and that stupid cat next door."

As for Sparky, he summed up his great thrill with Apollo by saying: "I think maybe people had a little better chance of identifying with the tremendous complexity of the flight by having such humorous names coming up all the time. If in some small way we helped to humanize everything, to give a little lightness to the extremely dangerous and daring flight, to perhaps make it just slightly easier for the astronauts and the people watching, then I'm proud of what we were able to do."

Of the hundreds of tributes that Sparky has received, I believe that the citation from St. Mary's College of California, on the day Sparky received his honorary Doctor of Humane Letters Degree, summarizes these past two decades best of all:

"Charles Monroe Schulz—well known as cartoonist, satirist, lucid yet compassionate interpreter of the human condition, you have been called, as well, teacher, psychiatrist,

poet—even theologian; although you have never pursued formal study at college or university, your work adorns the walls of faculty offices and student dormitories throughout the land. Philosophers, psychologists, preachers and professors of poetry find in your images the inspiration and embodiment of their insights. Your productions are examined, analyzed, attacked and praised by the studious at home and abroad.

"But your refusal to abandon the humble and genial ambition of drawing 'Funny pictures' has preserved you from the confinement of the academy. The figures of your imagination have engraved themselves upon the popular mind; the names of your characters have entered the common speech;

you have given new life and meaning to the phrase, 'Good Grief!' . . .

. . . "Employing, like other great artists, the simplest and most common materials, you have reduced the tangled illusions of adult existence to their naked paradigm: the fears, aspirations, angers and comforts of childhood. ('Children,' you have said, 'are caricatures of adults.') From these you have wrought, out of a warmth of heart so exigent that some have confused it with cruelty, an authentic, witty, compelling vision of modern life enmeshed in the perennial paradoxes of the human spirit. You have joined the select company of those who have made forms of popular entertainment the vehicle of enduring poetry.

"Although neither your hand nor your

imagination have ever suffered from the didactic cramp, it is not without reason that many have heard in your work some echoes of that Good News to which you have been so attentive yourself. The precisely rendered darkness and light of your fictive world seem at times to reflect, if modestly, a light which is not of this world. You are undeniably a realist; we salute you also as a Christian realist.

"Saint Mary's College of California takes pleasure today in conferring upon you the honorary degree of Doctor of Humane Letters."

Brother T. Michael, F.S.C.
President
Saint Mary's College of California.

While filming a sequence for the documentary on *Charlie Brown and Charlie Schulz*, we were shooting Joyce and Sparky bowling. Another lady bowler, attracted by the cameras and lights, came over and asked me: "Is this for television?" When I replied that it was, she said: "Well, why don't you come over and film my husband? He can bowl better than Mr. Schulz."

Similarly, many of the local townspeople consider Sparky just another "working stiff" and either are not impressed by or do not realize the worldwide impact of his work.

This anonymity of cartoonists in general is an interesting phenomenon: although the top comic strips are read by up to 100 million people, very few of the cartoonists (Al Capp being a major exception) are recognizable to the general public.

One exception to that rule, as far as Sparky is concerned, is the Oakland Ice Arena, where he is a weekly visitor and fan of the Oakland Seals, and where fans come over to Sparky for autographs. It is significant that he usually draws a sketch of one of the characters, in addition to the usual signing of his name, and perhaps this is one of the keys to his great success: he simply loves to draw . . . to create funny pictures . . . to entertain . . . even with an autograph. He is at once an artist, a humorist, and a philosopher, but it is his sense of humor—both professionally and socially—which seems to set him apart.

His ability to see, simply, "the funny side" of life along with the bitterness of life is a revolutionary combination as far as the comic strips are concerned. And added to his love for drawing and great sense of humor is his great competitiveness— not simply for "winning" but for doing his best at whatever he attempts, whether it be cartooning or golf or any competitive endeavor.

He is a quietly religious man, who believes the best way he can repay the "gift" he has been given is by trying to do the very best at his profession.

Perhaps the best description of his feelings came in something he wrote for the *Saturday Review*:

Drawing a daily comic strip is not unlike having an English theme hanging over your head every day for the rest of your life. I was never very good at writing those English themes in high school, and I usually put them off until the last minute. The only thing that saves me in trying to keep up with a comic strip schedule is the fact that it is quite a bit more enjoyable.

I am really a comic strip fanatic and always have been. When I was growing up in St. Paul, Minnesota, we subscribed to both local newspapers and always made sure that we went to the drugstore on Saturday night to buy the Minneapolis Sunday papers so that we would be able to read every comic published in the area. At that time, I was a great fan of Buck Rogers, Popeye, and Skippy.

After high school, I had a job delivering packages around the downtown St. Paul area, and I used to enjoy walking by the windows of the St. Paul *Pioneer Press* and watching the Sunday comics as they came rolling off the presses. It was my dream, of course, that one day my own comic strip would be included.

Almost twenty years have gone by since I first began drawing Charlie Brown and Snoopy, and I find that I still enjoy drawing them as much as I ever did, but, strangely enough, one of my greatest joys is gaining an extra week on the schedule. I have walked away from the post office many times with a tremendous feeling of joy, knowing that I have mailed in six strips that I thought were really good and that I have gained a week on that oppressive schedule.

During these twenty years, I have had the opportunity to observe what makes a good comic strip. I am convinced that the ones that have survived and maintained a high degree of quality are those which have a format that allows the creator room to express every idea that comes to him. A comic strip should have a very broad keyboard and should certainly not be a one- or two-note affair. If you are going to survive, you simply have to make use of every thought and every experience which have come to you.

A comic strip also has to grow. The only way you can stay ahead of your imitators is to search out new territories. Also, what is funny in a comic strip today will not necessarily be funny the following week. A good example of this is the character of Snoopy. The mere fact that we could read Snoopy's thoughts was funny in itself when *Peanuts* first began. Now, of course, it is the content of those thoughts that is important, and as he progresses in his imagination to new personalities, some of the things which he originally did as an ordinary dog would no longer be funny. Snoopy's personality in the strip has to be watched very carefully, for it can get away from me. Control over such a character requires a certain degree of common sense. I also believe that a comic strip, like a novel, should introduce the reader to new areas of thought and endeavor; these areas should be treated in an authentic manner. I never draw about anything unless I feel that I have a better than average knowledge of my subject. This does not mean that I am an expert on Beethoven, kite-flying, or psychiatry, but it means that as a creative person, I have the ability to skim the surface of such subjects and use just what I need.

Many times people come up to me and tell me how much they appreciate the philosophy of *Peanuts*. This never fails to confuse me, for I really do not know what this philosophy is. It has always seemed to me that the strip has a rather bitter feeling to it, and it certainly deals in defeat. It has given me the opportunity to express many of my own thoughts about life and people. It is my own opinion that it is absolutely necessary for each one of us to strive to gain emotional maturity. Unless a person becomes mature in all things, he will always have fears and anxieties plaguing him. It is interesting to put these adult fears and anxieties into the conversations of the children in *Peanuts*. The passage of time is an area that will almost always show up a person's immaturity. Children have a strange attitude toward time, for they do not have the patience to wait for days to pass. They want what they want immediately, and adults who are incapable of learning to wait for things will find themselves in all sorts of trouble.

It is also immature not to be able to realize that things that are going to happen in the future are quite often inevitable. If children are allowed to do so, they will put off almost anything, merely because it is in the future; of course, adults will do the same.

I am asked quite frequently to attempt to analyze each of the characters in the strip, but I find myself incapable of doing this. I really cannot talk about Charlie Brown, Linus, or Lucy as individuals. I can draw them, and I can think of things for them to do, but I do not talk well about them.

One thing that does interest me, however, is the set of offstage characters I have gradually accumulated. A reader once wrote to me and gave a fairly good description of what he thought Peppermint Patty's father must be like. This offstage parent refers to his daughter as a "rare gem," and apparently tolerates her tomboyishness quite well. The reader speculated that her father has either divorced his wife or perhaps she has died. I have treated Charlie Brown's father in a fair amount of detail, because I have let it be known that he is very receptive to his son's impromptu visits to the barber shop. Most of this is autobiographical, for my dad always greeted me cordially when I would drop in at his barber shop, and I used to go there and sit and read the newspapers and magazines until he closed his shop in the evening. He also never objected if I rang the NO SALE button on the cash register and removed a nickel for a candy bar.

Linus's mother seems to be the peculiar one. As Charlie Brown once remarked, "I am beginning to understand why you drag that blanket around." She seems to be obsessed with his doing well in school, and tries to spur him on by sneaking notes into his lunch which read, "Study hard today. Your father and I are very proud of you and want you to get a good education."

Some of the offstage characters reach a point where they could never be drawn. I think the little redheaded girl is a lot like the inside of Snoopy's doghouse. Each of us can imagine what she must look like much better than I could ever draw her, and I am sure that every reader sees a different doghouse interior and would be a little disappointed if I were to attempt to draw it in detail.

Linus's beloved Miss Othmar, his teacher, is a rather strange person, and I have tried to do much with her through the conversation of Linus. I have experimented with a two-level story line at times. I have tried to show Linus's view of what is happening at school, but then show what actually was occurring. I have done this to bring out a truth I have observed, and this is that children see more than we think they do, but at the same time almost never seem to know what is going on. This is an interesting paradox, and one with which adults should try to acquaint themselves, if they are going to deal well with children.

I am very proud of the comic strip medium and am never ashamed to admit that I draw a comic strip. I do not regard it as great art, but I have always felt it is certainly on the level with other entertainment mediums which are part of the so-called "popular arts." In many ways, I do not think we have realized the potential of the comic strip, but sometimes I feel it is too late. Many regard the comic page as a necessary evil and a nuisance, but it is there and it helps sell newspapers. With a little more tolerance and with a little more dedication on the part of those who create the comics, perhaps we could do better. I look back upon great features such as *Out Our Way*, and I feel that perhaps we can never recapture some of that glory. I really shudder when I read a description of a new feature about to be launched by some newspaper syndicate and they refer to it as "off-beat." It is time we have some new features which are "on-beat," and which are about real people doing real things.

Epilogue

One December evening in 1969, in New York City, Charlie Brown simultaneously played before (a) a sellout crowd for the stage show, (b) a sellout audience for the Feature at the Radio City Music Hall, and (c) a repeat network television special (*A Charlie Brown Christmas*) that was also seen by fifty-five million other Americans across the country. No performer in the history of show business can make that statement.

I guess in the final analysis, millions of us follow Charlie Brown . . . millions of us cheer him on . . . because his many struggles represent so many of our own individual struggles.

So we're right out there on the mound with him every day.

And I can't think of a more exciting place to be.

Credits